Demosthenes' *On the Crown*

STUDIES IN SPEECH

CONSULTING EDITOR

Don Geiger
University of California, Berkeley

Demosthenes'
On the Crown

A Critical Case Study of a Masterpiece of Ancient Oratory

EDITED BY

James J. Murphy
University of California, Davis

WITH A NEW TRANSLATION BY

John J. Keaney
Princeton University

RANDOM HOUSE
New York

CONTENTS

Introduction

by James J. Murphy

As Charles Rann Kennedy has observed of Demosthenes' speech *On the Crown,* "This has justly been considered the greatest speech of the greatest orator in the world."

This type of praise has been given to the oration for almost twenty-four centuries. Even his opponent, Aeschines, who was exiled by his defeat in this famous case, later praised the speech to the students he was instructing on the Isle of Rhodes. The story is told that he had been declaiming his own Crown speech to the students, who marveled that such a fine performance could still have gained fewer than one-fifth of the votes—the minimum necessary by Athenian law to avoid banishment in such cases. "But oh," Aeschines said, "if only you had heard Demosthenes!"

The Roman orator Cicero was so enchanted by the speech that he translated it into Latin together with that of Aeschines. Unfortunately his translation has not survived, but in his introduction to the translation (*De optimo genere oratorum—The Best Kind of Orator*) he declares that "nothing can be imagined more inspired than the orator Demosthenes." The Roman schoolmaster Quintilian praised him also, making him one of the recommended model orators in his *Institutes of Oratory*.

Medieval and Renaissance scholars admired the speech, even to the point of manufacturing spurious decrees, letters, and other documents to which Demosthenes refers throughout the oration. These documents have been lost since ancient times, so that even the main indictment itself has had to be reconstructed by modern scholars. Thus it is an index of their interest that medieval readers began the practice of insertions to make what they regarded as a more complete text.

The speech was first published separately in 1521, and throughout early modern times enjoyed the esteem of such educators as Melancthon. The English scholar Roger Ascham, in fact, met regularly with Queen Elizabeth to read the works of Demosthenes. Later Henry, Lord Brougham, a prominent English rhetorical critic, made the orator a prime example of successful oratory. In the United States Demosthenes was heralded by such men as Chauncey Goodrich in his Yale lectures from 1822 onward.

During the early part of this century the stresses of World War I spurred still another revival of interest. Admired by the French for his staunch resistance to the invading Macedonians, he was eulogized as a patriot by Georges Clemenceau. Some German writers, on the other hand, saw in him the perfection of political power. Aside from these views, however, there is a growing stream of serious scholarly work devoted to the career and speeches of a man who was in a sense the last spokesman of a free Athens.

This volume, then, is offered to enable the modern reader to understand and then to appreciate the oratorical artistry of Demosthenes. There are many lessons to be learned from a careful reading of his oration *On the Crown*—historical, moral, political, rhetorical—and the essays in the volume are offered as guides to such study. A fresh translation in the modern idiom was created especially for this book by Professor John J. Keaney of the Department of Classics of Princeton University. This text, the speech itself, is of course the core of any reader's study. Yet the speech cannot come alive to the reader unless he can also gain some understanding of the historical situation, the accusations of Aeschines, Demosthenes' adroit use of arguments, his deft phrasing, and the basic appeal he makes to his fellow citizens in a time of crisis.

Part One of the book deals with the historical situation and the speech itself. Plutarch's *Life of Demosthenes* sets forth the main elements of his career, as it was understood in ancient times, while the modern survey of Professor George Kennedy outlines the major speeches that had brought Demosthenes into prominence before his accusation by Aeschines. The translation itself is preceded by a brief discussion of Aeschines' strategy in his own speech of attack against Demosthenes.

Part Two opens with a brief resumé of the rhetorical factors to be considered in evaluating any speech. This essay by Professor Jon Ericson outlines both the function and the process of speech criticism, as a guide to the reader's own assessment of Demosthenes' work. The reader will note at once that a complete critical evaluation of any one speech—let alone a masterpiece like Demosthenes'—is a task demanding great skill. A contemporary of Demosthenes, Aristotle, defines rhetoric as the ability to discover all available means of persuasion in a given set of circumstances. While this sets a very high standard for the critical reader of *On the Crown,* the four essays on structure, history, argument, and language which complete Part Two hopefully will provide indications of how to achieve that high standard.

It is, after all, almost a definition of a masterpiece that new readers keep finding fresh insights into a work of art.

With such a many-faceted approach to the speech, the reader may come to understand why this has been called a true masterpiece in the history of oratory.

PART ONE

Demosthenes and His Greatest Speech

The Life of Demosthenes

by Plutarch

Demosthenes, the father of Demosthenes, was a citizen of good rank and quality, as Theopompus informs us, surnamed the Sword-maker, because he had a large workhouse, and kept servants skilful in that art of work. But of that which Aeschines the orator said of his mother, that she was descended of one Gylon, who fled his country upon an accusation of treason, and of a barbarian woman, I can affirm nothing, whether he spoke true, or slandered and maligned her. This is certain, that Demosthenes, being as yet but seven years old, was left by his father in affluent circumstances, the whole value of his estate being little short of fifteen talents, and that he was wronged by his guardians, part of his fortune being embezzled by them, and the rest neglected; insomuch that even his teachers were defrauded of their salaries. This was the reason that he did not obtain the liberal education that he should have had; besides that, on account of weakness and delicate health, his mother would not let him exert himself, and his teachers forbore to urge him. He was meagre and sickly from the first, and hence

From *Plutarch, The Lives of the Noble Grecians and Romans,* translated by John Dryden and revised by Arthur Hugh Clough (New York: Modern Library), pp. 1024–1040.

had his nickname of Batalus given him, it is said, by the boys, in derision of his appearance; Batalus being, as some tell us, a certain enervated flute-player, in ridicule of whom Antiphanes wrote a play. Others speak of Batalus as a writer of wanton verses and drinking songs. And it would seem that some part of the body, not decent to be named, was at that time called *batalus* by the Athenians. But the name of Argas, which also they say was a nickname of Demosthenes, was given him for his behavior, as being savage and spiteful, *argas* being one of the poetical words for a snake; or for his disagreeable way of speaking, Argas being the name of a poet who composed very harshly and disagreeably. So much, as Plato says, for such matters.

The first occasion of his eager inclination to oratory, they say, was this. Callistratus, the orator, being to plead in open court for Oropus, the expectation of the issue of that cause was very great, as well for the ability of the orator, who was then at the height of his reputation, as also for the fame of the action itself. Therefore, Demosthenes, having heard the tutors and school-masters agreeing among themselves to be present at this trial, with much importunity persuaded his tutor to take him along with him to the hearing; who, having some acquaintance with the doorkeepers, procured a place where the boy might sit unseen, and hear what was said. Callistratus having got the day, and being much admired, the boy began to look upon his glory with a kind of emulation, observing how he was courted on all hands, and attended on his way by the multitude; but his wonder was more than all excited by the power of his eloquence, which seemed able to subdue and win over anything. From this time, therefore, bidding farewell to other sorts of learning and study, he now began to exercise himself, and to take pains in declaiming, as one that meant to be himself also an orator. He made use of Isæus as his guide to the art of speaking, though Isocrates at that time was giving lessons; whether, as some say, because he was an orphan, and was not able to pay Isocrates his appointed fee of ten minæ, or because he preferred Isæus's speaking, as being more businesslike and effective in actual use. Hermippus says that he met with certain memoirs without any author's name, in which it was written that Demosthenes was a scholar to Plato, and learnt much of his eloquence from him; and he also mentions Ctesibius, as reporting from Callias of Syracuse and some others, that Demosthenes secretly obtained a knowledge of the systems of Isocrates and Alcidamas, and mastered them thoroughly.

As soon, therefore, as he was grown up to man's estate, he began to go to law with his guardians, and to write orations against them; who, in the meantime, had recourse to various subterfuges and pleas for new trials, and Demosthenes, though he was thus, as Thucydides says, taught his business in dangers, and by his own exertions was successful in his suit, was yet unable for all this to recover so much as a small fraction of his patrimony. He only attained some degree of confidence in speaking, and some competent experience in it. And having got a taste of the honor and power which are acquired by pleadings, he now ventured to come forth, and to undertake public business. And, as it is said of Laomedon, the Orchomenian, that, by advice of his physician, he used to run long distances to keep off some disease of his spleen, and by that means having, through labor and exercise, framed the habit of his body, he betook himself to the great garland games, and became one of the best runners at the long race; so it happened to Demosthenes, who, first venturing upon oratory for the recovery of his own private property, by this acquired ability in speaking, and at length, in public business, as it were in the great games, came to have the pre-eminence of all competitors in the assembly. But when he first addressed himself to the people, he met with great discouragements, and was derided for his strange and uncouth style, which was cumbered with long sentences and tortured with formal arguments to a most harsh and disagreeable excess. Besides, he had, it seems, a weakness in his voice, a perplexed and indistinct utterance and a shortness of breath, which, by breaking and disjointing his sentences, much obscured the sense and meaning of what he spoke. So that in the end being quite disheartened, he forsook the assembly; and as he was walking carelessly and sauntering about the Piræus, Eunomus, the Thriasian, then a very old man, seeing him, upbraided him, saying that his diction was very much like that of Pericles, and that he was wanting to himself through cowardice and meanness of spirit, neither bearing up with courage against popular outcry, nor fitting his body for action, but suffering it to languish through mere sloth and negligence.

Another time, when the assembly had refused to hear him, and he was going home with his head muffled up, taking it very heavily, they relate that Satyrus, the actor, followed him, and being his familiar acquaintance, entered into conversation with him. To whom, when Demosthenes bemoaned himself, that having been the most industrious of all the pleaders, and having almost spent the whole strength and vigor of his body in that employment, he could not yet find any acceptance with the people, that drunken sots, mariners, and illiterate fellows were heard, and had the hustings for their own, while he himself was despised, "You say true, Demosthenes," replied Satyrus, "but I will quickly remedy the cause of all this, if you will repeat to me some passage out of Euripides or Sophocles." Which when Demosthenes had pronounced, Satyrus presently taking it up after him, gave the same passage, in his rendering of it, such a new form, by accompanying it with the proper mien and gesture, that to Demosthenes it seemed quite another thing. By this, being convinced how much grace and ornament language acquires from action, he began to esteem it a small matter, and as good as nothing for a man to exercise himself in declaiming, if he neglected enunciation and delivery. Hereupon he built himself a place to study in under ground (which was still remaining in our time), and hither he would come constantly every day to form his action and to exercise his voice; and here he would continue, oftentimes without intermission, two or three months together, shaving one half of his head, that so for shame he might not go abroad, though he desired it ever so much.

Nor was this all, but he also made his conversation with people abroad, his common speech, and his business, subservient to his studies, taking from hence occasions and arguments as matter to work upon. For as soon as he was parted from his company, down he would go at once into his study, and run over everything in order that had passed, and the reasons that might be alleged for and against it. Any speeches, also, that he was present at, he would go over again with himself, and reduce into periods; and whatever others spoke to him, or he to them, he would correct, transform, and vary several ways. Hence it was that he was looked upon as a person of no great natural genius, but one who owed all the power and ability he had in speaking to labor and industry. Of the truth of which it was thought to be no small sign that he was very rarely heard to speak upon the occasion, but though he were by name frequently called upon by the people, as he sat in the assembly, yet he would not rise unless he had previously considered the subject, and came prepared for it. So that many of the popular pleaders used to make it a jest against him; and Pytheas once, scoffing at him, said that his arguments smelt of the lamp. To which Demosthenes gave the sharp answer, "It is true, indeed, Pytheas, that your lamp and mine are not conscious of the same things." To others, however, he would not much deny it, but would admit frankly enough, that he neither entirely wrote his speeches beforehand, nor yet spoke wholly extempore. And he would affirm that it was the more truly popular act to use premeditation, such preparation being a kind of respect to the people; whereas, to slight and take no care how what is said is likely to be received by the audience, shows something of an oligarchical temper, and is the course of one that intends force rather than persuasion. Of his want of courage and assurance to speak offhand, they make it also another argument that, when he was at a loss and discomposed, Demades would often rise up on the sudden to support him, but he was never observed to do the same for Demades.

Whence then, may some say, was it, that Aeschines speaks of him as a person so much to be wondered at for his boldness in speaking? Or, how could it be, when Python, the Byzantine, with so much confidence and such a torrent of words inveighed against the Athenians, that Demosthenes alone stood up to oppose him? Or when Lamarchus, the Myrinæan, had written a panegyric upon King Philip and Alexander, in which he uttered many things in reproach of the Thebans and Olynthians, and at the Olympic Games recited it publicly, how was it that he, rising up, and recounting historically and demonstratively what benefits and advantages all Greece had received from the Thebans and Chalcidians, and, on the contrary, what mischiefs the flatterers of the Macedonians had brought upon it, so turned the minds of all that were present that the sophist, in alarm at the outcry against him, secretly made his way out of the assembly? But Demosthenes, it should seem, regarded other points in the character of Pericles to be unsuited to him; but his reserve and his sustained manner, and his forbearing to speak on the sudden, or upon every occasion, as being the things to which principally he owed his greatness, these he followed, and endeavored to imitate, neither wholly neglecting the glory which present occasion offered, nor yet willing too often to expose his faculty to the mercy of chance. For, in fact, the orations which were spoken by him had much more of boldness and confidence in them than those that he wrote, if we may believe Eratosthenes, Demetrius the Phalerian, and the Comedians. Eratosthenes says that often in his speaking he would be transported into a kind of ecstasy, and Demetrius, that he uttered the famous metrical adjuration to the people—

"By the earth, the springs, the rivers, and the streams,"

as a man inspired and beside himself. One of the comedians calls him a *rhopoperperethras*, and another scoffs at him for his use of antithesis:—

"And what he took, took back; a phrase to please,
The very fancy of Demosthenes."

Unless, indeed, this also is meant by Antiphanes for a jest upon the speech on Halonesus, which Demosthenes advised the Athenians not to *take* at Philip's hands, but to *take back*.

All, however, used to consider Demades, in the mere use of his natural gifts, an orator impossible to surpass, and that in what he spoke on the sudden, he excelled all the study and preparation of Demosthenes. And Ariston, the Chian, has recorded a judgment which Theophrastus passed upon the orators; for being asked what kind of orator he accounted Demosthenes, he answered, "Worthy of the city of Athens;" and then what he thought of Demades, he answered, "Above it." And the same philosopher reports that Polyeuctus, the Sphettian, one of the Athenian politicians about that time, was wont to say that Demosthenes was the greatest orator, but Phocion the ablest, as he expressed the most sense in the fewest words. And, indeed, it is related that Demosthenes himself, as often as Phocion stood up to plead against him, would say to his acquaintance, "Here comes the knife to my speech." Yet it does not appear whether he had this feeling for his powers of speaking, or for his life and character, and meant to say that one word or nod from a man who was really trusted would go further than a thousand lengthy periods from others.

Demetrius, the Phalerian, tells us that he was informed by Demosthenes himself, now grown old, that the ways he made use of to remedy his natural bodily infirmities and defects were such as these; his inarticulate and stammering pronunciation he overcame and rendered more distinct by speaking with pebbles in his mouth; his voice he disciplined by declaiming and reciting speeches or verses when he was out of breath, while running or going up steep places; and that in his house he had a large looking-glass, before which he would stand and go through his exercises. It is told that some one once came to request his assistance as a pleader, and related how he had been assaulted and beaten. "Certainly," said Demosthenes, "nothing of the kind can have happened to you." Upon which the other, raising his voice, exclaimed loudly, "What, Demosthenes, nothing has been done to me?" "Ah," replied Demosthenes, "now I hear the voice of one that has been injured and beaten." Of so great consequence towards the gaining of belief did he esteem the tone and action of the speaker. The action which he used himself was wonderfully pleasing to the common people, but by well-educated people, as, for example, by Demetrius, the Phalerian, it was looked upon as mean, humiliating, and unmanly. And Hermippus says of Aesion, that, being asked his opinion concerning the ancient orators, and those of his own time, he answered that it was admirable to see with what composure and in what high style they addressed themselves to the people; but that the orations of Demosthenes, when they are read, certainly appear to be superior in point of construction, and more effective. His written speeches, beyond all question, are characterized by austere tone and by their severity. In his extempore retorts and rejoinders, he allowed himself the use of jest and mockery. When Demades said, "Demosthenes teach me! So might the sow teach Minerva!" he replied, "Was it this Minerva, that was lately found playing the harlot in Collytus?" When a thief, who had the nickname of the Brazen, was attempting to upbraid him for sitting up late, and writing by candle-light, "I know very well," said he, "that you had rather have all lights out; and wonder not, O ye men of Athens, at the many robberies which are committed, since we have thieves of brass and walls of clay." But on these points, though we have much more to mention, we will add nothing at present. We will proceed to take an estimate of his character from his actions and his life as a statesman.

His first entering into public business was much about the time of the Phocian war, as himself affirms, and may be collected from his Philippic orations. For of these, some were made after that action was over, and the earliest of them refer to its concluding events. It is certain that' he engaged in the accusation of Midias when he was but two-and-thirty years old, having as yet no interest or reputation as a politician. And this it was, I consider, that induced him to withdraw the action, and accept a sum of money as a compromise. For of himself—

"He was no easy or good-natured man,"

but of a determined disposition, and resolute to see himself righted; however, finding it a hard matter and above his strength to deal with Midias, a man so well secured on all sides with money, eloquence, and friends, he yielded to the entreaties of those who interceded for him. But had he seen any hopes or possibility of prevailing, I cannot believe that three thousand drachmas could have taken off the edge of his revenge. The object which he chose for himself in the commonwealth was noble and just, the defense of the Grecians against Philip; and in this he behaved himself so worthily that he soon grew famous, and excited attention everywhere for his eloquence and courage in speaking. He was admired through all Greece, the King of Persia courted him, and by Philip himself he was more esteemed than all the other orators. His very enemies were forced to confess that they had to do with a man of mark; for such a character even Aeschines and Hyperides give him, where they accuse and speak against him.

So that I cannot imagine what ground Theopompus had to say that Demosthenes was of a fickle, unsettled disposition, and could not long continue firm either to the same men or the same affairs; whereas the contrary is most apparent, for the same party and post in politics which he held from the beginning, to these he kept constant to the end; and was so far from leaving them while he lived that he chose rather to forsake his life than his purpose. He was never heard to apologize for shifting sides like Demades, who would say he often spoke against himself, but never against the city; nor as Melanopus, who, being generally against Callistratus, but being often bribed off with money, was wont to tell the people, "The man indeed is my enemy, but we must submit for the good of our country;" nor again as Nicodemus, the Messenian, who having first appeared on Cassander's side, and afterwards taken part with Demetrius, said the two things were not in themselves contrary, it being always most advisable to obey the conqueror. We have nothing of this kind to say against Demosthenes, as one who would turn aside or prevaricate, either in word or deed. There could not have been less variation in his public acts if they had all been played, so to say, from first to last, from the same score. Panætius, the philosopher, said that most of his orations are so written as if they were to prove this one conclusion, that what is honest and virtuous is for itself only to be chosen; as that of the Crown, that against Aristocrates, that for the Immunities, and the Philippics; in all which he persuades his fellow-citizens to pursue not that which seems most pleasant, easy, or profitable; but declares, over and over again, that they ought in the first place to prefer that which is just and honorable before their own safety and preservation. So that if he had kept his hands clean, if his courage for the wars had been answerable to the generosity of his principles, and the dignity of his orations, he might deservedly have his name placed, not in the number of such orators as Mœrocles, Polyeuctus, and Hyperides, but in the highest rank with Cimon, Thucydides, and Pericles.

Certainly amongst those who were contemporary with him, Phocion, though he appeared on the less commendable side in the commonwealth, and was counted as one of the Macedonian party, nevertheless, by his courage and his honesty, procured himself a name not inferior to these of Ephialtes, Aristides, and Cimon. But Demosthenes, being neither fit to be relied on for courage in arms, as Demetrius says, nor on all sides inaccessible to bribery (for how invincible soever he was against the gifts of Philip and the Macedonians, yet elsewhere he lay open to assault, and was overpowered by the gold which came down from Susa and Ecbatana), was therefore esteemed better able to recommend than to imitate the virtues of past times. And yet (excepting only Phocion), even in his life and manners, he far surpassed the other orators of his time. None of them addressed the people so boldly; he attacked the faults, and opposed himself to the unreasonable desires of the multitude, as may be seen in his orations. Theopompus writes, that the Athenians having by name selected Demosthenes, and called upon him to accuse a certain person, he refused to do it; upon which the assembly being all in an uproar, he rose up and said, "Your counsellor, whether you will or no, O ye men of Athens, you shall always have me; but a sycophant or false accuser, though you would have me, I shall never be." And his conduct in the case of Antiphon was perfectly aristocratical; whom, after he had been acquitted in the assembly, he took and brought before the court of Areopagus, and, setting at naught the displeasure of the people, convicted him there of having promised Philip to burn the arsenal; whereupon the man was condemned by that court, and suffered for it. He accused, also, Theoris, the priestess, amongst other misdemeanors, of having instructed and taught the slaves to deceive and cheat their masters, for which the sentence of death was passed upon her, and she was executed.

The oration which Apollodorus made use of, and by it carried the cause against Timotheus, the general, in an action of debt, it is said was written for him by Demosthenes; as also those against Phormion and Stephanus, in which latter case he was thought to have acted dishonorably, for the speech which Phormion used against Apollodorus was also of his making; he, as it were, having simply furnished two adversaries out of the same shop with weapons to wound one another. Of his orations addressed to the public assemblies, that against Androtion, and those against Timocrates and Aristocrates, were written for others, before he had come forward himself as a politician. They were composed, it seems, when he was but seven or eight and twenty years old. That against Aristogiton, and that for the Immunities, he spoke himself, at the request, as he says, of Ctesippus, the son of Chabrias, but, as some say, out of courtship to the young man's mother. Though, in fact, he did not marry her, for his wife was a woman of Samos, as Demetrius, the Magnesian, writes, in his book on Persons of the same Name. It is not certain whether his oration against Aeschines, for Misconduct as Ambassador, was ever spoken; although Idomeneus says that Aeschines wanted only thirty voices to condemn him. But this seems not to be correct, at least so far as may be conjectured from both their orations concerning the Crown; for in these, neither of them speaks clearly or directly of it, as a cause that ever came to trial. But let others decide this controversy.

It was evident, even in time of peace, what course Demosthenes would steer in the commonwealth; for whatever was done by the Macedonian, he criticized and found fault with, and upon all occasions was stirring up the people of Athens, and inflaming them against him. Therefore, in the court of Philip, no man was so much talked of, or of so great account as he; and when he came thither, one of the ten ambassadors who were sent into Macedonia, though all had audience given them, yet his speech was answered with most care and exactness. But in other respects, Philip entertained him not so honorably as the rest, neither did he show him the same kindness and civility with which he applied himself to the party of Aeschines and Philocrates. So that, when the others commended Philip for his able speaking, his beautiful person, nay, and also for his good companionship in drinking, Demosthenes could not refrain from cavilling at these praises; the first, he said, was a quality which might well enough become a rhetorician, the second a woman, and the last was only the property of a sponge; no one of them was the proper commendation of a prince.

But when things came at last to war, Philip on the one side being not able to live in peace, and the Athenians, on the other side, being stirred up by Demosthenes, the first action he put them upon was the reducing of Eubœa, which, by the treachery of the tyrants, was brought under subjection to Philip. And on his proposition, the decree was voted, and they crossed over thither and chased the Macedonians out of the island. The next was the relief of the Byzantines and Perinthians, whom the Macedonians at that time were attacking. He persuaded the people to lay aside their enmity against these cities, to forget the offenses committed by them in the Confederate War, and to send them such succors as eventually saved and secured them. Not long after, he undertook an embassy through the states of Greece, which he solicited and so far incensed against Philip that, a few only excepted, he brought them all into a general league. So that, besides the forces composed of the citizens themselves, there was an army consisting of fifteen thousand foot and two thousand horse, and the money to pay these strangers was levied and brought in with great cheerfulness. On which occasion it was, says Theophrastus, on the allies requesting that their contributions for the war might be ascertained and stated, Crobylus, the orator, made use of the saying, "War can't be fed at so much a day." Now was all Greece up in arms, and in great expectation what would be the event. The Eubœans, the Achæans, the Corinthians, the Megarians, the Leucadians, and Corcyræans, their people and their cities, were all joined together in a league. But the hardest task was yet behind, left for Demosthenes, to draw the Thebans into this confederacy with the rest. Their country bordered next upon Attica, they had great forces for the war, and at that time they were accounted the best soldiers of all Greece, but it was no easy matter to make them break with Philip, who, by many good offices, had so lately obliged them in the Phocian war; especially considering how the subjects of dispute and variance between the two cities were continually renewed and exasperated by petty quarrels, arising out of the proximity of their frontiers.

But after Philip, being now grown high and puffed up with his good success at Amphissa, on a sudden surprised Elatea and possessed himself of Phocis, and the Athenians were in a great consternation, none durst venture to rise up to speak, no one knew what to say, all were at a loss, and the whole assembly in silence and perplexity, in this extremity of affairs Demosthenes was the only man who appeared, his counsel to them being alliance with the Thebans. And having in other ways encouraged the people, and, as his manner was, raised their spirits up with hopes, he, with some others, was sent ambassador to Thebes. To oppose him, as Marsyas says, Philip also sent thither his envoys, Amyntas and Clearchus, two Macedonians, besides Daochus, a Thessalian, and Thrasydæus. Now the Thebans, in their consultations, were well enough aware what suited best with their own interest, but every one had before his eyes the terrors of war, and their losses in the Phocian troubles were still recent: but such was the force and power of the orator, fanning up, as Theopompus says, their courage, and firing their emulation, that, casting away every thought of prudence, fear, or obligation, in a sort of divine possession, they chose the path of honor, to which his words invited them. And this success, thus accomplished by an orator, was thought to be so glorious and of such consequence, that Philip immediately sent heralds to treat and petition for a peace: all Greece was aroused, and up in arms to help. And the commanders-in-chief, not only of Attica, but of Bœotia, applied themselves to Demosthenes, and observed his directions. He managed all the assemblies of the Thebans, no less than those of the Athenians; he was beloved both by the one and by the other, and exercised the same supreme authority with both; and that not by unfair means, or without just cause, as Theopompus professes, but indeed it was no more than was due to his merit.

But there was, it would seem, some divinely ordered fortune, commissioned, in the revolution of things, to put a period at this time to the liberty of Greece, which opposed and thwarted all their actions, and by many signs foretold what should happen. Such were the sad predictions uttered by the Pythian priestess, and this old oracle cited out of the Sibyl's verses: —

"The battle on Thermodon that shall be
  Safe at a distance I desire to see,

> Far, like an eagle, watching in the air,
> Conquered shall weep, and conqueror perish there."

This Thermodon, they say, is a little rivulet here in our country in Chæronea, running into the Cephisus. But we know of none that is so called at the present time; and can only conjecture that the streamlet which is now called Hæmon, and runs by the Temple of Hercules, where the Grecians were encamped, might perhaps in those days be called Thermodon, and after the fight, being filled with blood and dead bodies, upon this occasion, as we guess, might change its old name for that which it now bears. Yet Duris says that this Thermodon was no river, but that some of the soldiers, as they were pitching their tents and digging trenches about them, found a small stone statue, which, by the inscription, appeared to be the figure of Thermodon, carrying a wounded Amazon in his arms; and that there was another oracle current about it, as follows:—

> "The battle on Thermodon that shall be,
> Fail not, black raven, to attend and see;
> The flesh of men shall there abound for thee."

In fine, it is not easy to determine what is the truth. But of Demosthenes it is said that he had such great confidence in the Grecian forces, and was so excited by the sight of the courage and resolution of so many brave men ready to engage the enemy, that he would by no means endure they should give any heed to oracles, or hearken to prophecies, but gave out that he suspected even the prophetess herself, as if she had been tampered with to speak in favor of Philip. The Thebans he put in mind of Epaminondas, the Athenians of Pericles, who always took their own measures and governed their actions by reason, looking upon things of this kind as mere pretexts for cowardice. Thus far, therefore, Demosthenes acquitted himself like a brave man. But in the fight he did nothing honorable, nor was his performance answerable to his speeches. For he fled, deserting his place disgracefully, and throwing away his arms, not ashamed, as Pytheas observed, to belie the inscription written on his shield, in letters of gold, "With good fortune."

In the meantime Philip, in the first moment of victory, was so transported with joy, that he grew extravagant, and going out after he had drunk largely to visit the dead bodies, he chanted the first words of the decree that had been passed on the motion of Demosthenes—

"The motion of Demosthenes, Demosthenes's son,"

dividing it metrically into feet, and marking the beats.

But when he came to himself, and had well considered the danger he was lately under, he could not forbear from shuddering at the wonderful ability and power of an orator who had made him hazard his life and empire on the issue of a few brief hours. The fame of it also reached even to the court of Persia, and the king sent letters to his lieutenants commanding them to supply Demosthenes with money, and to pay every attention to him, as the only man of all the Grecians who was able to give Philip occupation and find employment for his forces near home, in the troubles of Greece. This afterwards came to the knowledge of Alexander, by certain letters of Demosthenes which he found at Sardis, and by other papers of the Persian officers, stating the large sums which had been given him.

At this time, however, upon the ill-success which now happened to the Grecians, those of the contrary faction in the commonwealth fell foul upon Demosthenes and took the opportunity to frame several informations and indictments against him. But the people not only acquitted him of these accusations, but continued towards him their former respect, and still invited him, as a man that meant well, to take a part in public affairs. Insomuch that when the bones of those who had been slain at Chæronea were brought home to be solemnly interred, Demosthenes was the man they chose to make the funeral oration. They did not show, under the misfortunes which befell them, a base or ignoble mind, as Theopompus writes in his exaggerated style, but on the contrary, by the honor and respect paid to their counsellor, they made it appear that they were no way dissatisfied with the counsels he had given them. The speech, therefore, was spoken by Demosthenes. But the subsequent decrees he would not allow to be passed in his own name, but made use of those of his friends, one after another, looking upon his own as unfortunate and inauspicious; till at length he took courage again after the death of Philip, who did not long outlive his victory at Chæronea. And this, it seems, was that which was foretold in the last verse of the oracle—

"Conquered shall weep, and conqueror perish there."

Demosthenes had secret intelligence of the death of Philip, and laying hold of this opportunity to prepossess the people with courage and better hopes for the future, he came into the assembly with a cheerful countenance, pretending to have had a dream that presaged some great good fortune for Athens; and, not long after, arrived the messengers who brought the news of Philip's death. No sooner had the people received it, but immediately they offered sacrifice to the gods, and decreed that Pausanias should be presented with a crown. Demosthenes appeared publicly in a rich dress, with a chaplet on his head, though it were but the seventh day since the death of his daughter, as is said by Aeschines, who upbraids him upon this account, and rails at him as one void of natural affection towards his children. Whereas, indeed, he rather betrays himself to be of a poor, low spirit, and effeminate mind, if he really means to make wailings and lamentation the only signs of a gentle and affectionate nature, and to condemn those who bear such accidents with more temper and less passion. For my own part, I cannot say that the behavior of the Athenians on this occasion was wise or honorable, to crown themselves with garlands and to sacrifice to the gods for the death of a prince who, in the midst of his success and victories, when they were a conquered people, had used them with so much clemency and humanity. For besides provoking fortune, it was a base thing, and unworthy in itself, to make him a citizen of Athens, and pay him honors while he lived, and yet as soon as he fell by another's hand, to set no bounds to their jollity, to insult over him dead, and to sing triumphant songs of victory, as if by their own valor they had vanquished him. I must at the same time commend the behavior of Demosthenes, who, leaving tears and lamentations and domestic sorrows to the women, made it his business to attend to the interests of the commonwealth. And I think it the duty of him who would be accounted to have a soul truly valiant, and fit for government, that, standing always firm to the common good, and letting private griefs and troubles find their compensation in public blessings, he should maintain the dignity of his character and station, much more than actors who represent the persons of kings and tyrants, who, we see, when they either laugh or weep on the stage, follow, not their own private inclinations, but the course consistent with the subject and with their position. And if, moreover, when our neighbor is in misfortune, it is not our duty to forbear offering any consolation, but rather to say whatever may tend to cheer him, and to invite his attention to any agreeable objects, just as we tell people who are troubled with sore eyes to withdraw their sight from bright and offensive colors to green, and those of a softer mixture, from whence can a man seek, in his own case, better arguments of consolation for afflictions in his family, than from the prosperity of his country, by making public and domestic chances count, so to say, together, and the better fortune of the state obscure and conceal the less happy circumstances of the individual. I have been induced to say so much, because I have known many readers melted by Aeschines's language into a soft and unmanly tenderness.

But now to turn to my narrative. The cities of Greece were inspirited once more by the efforts of Demosthenes to form a league together. The Thebans, whom he had provided with arms, set upon their garrison, and slew many of them; the Athenians made preparations to join their forces with them; Demosthenes ruled supreme in the popular assembly, and wrote letters to the Persian officers who commanded under the king in Asia, inciting them to make war upon the Macedonian, calling him child and simpleton. But as soon as Alexander had settled matters in his own country, and came in person with his army into Bœotia, down fell the courage of the Athenians, and Demosthenes was hushed; the Thebans, deserted by them, fought by themselves, and lost their city. After which, the people of Athens, all in distress and great perplexity, resolved to send ambassadors to Alexander, and amongst others, made choice of Demosthenes for one: but his heart failing him for fear of the king's anger, he returned back from Cithæron, and left the embassy. In the meantime, Alexander sent to Athens, requiring ten of their orators to be delivered up to him, as Idomeneus and Duris have reported, but as the most and best historians say, he demanded these eight only,—Demosthenes, Polyeuctus, Ephialtes, Lycurgus, Mœrocles, Demon, Callisthenes, and Charidemus. It was upon this occasion that Demosthenes related to them the fable in which the sheep are said to deliver up their dogs to the wolves; himself and those who with him contended for the people's safety being, in his comparison, the dogs that defended the flock, and Alexander "the Macedonian arch-wolf." He further told them, "As we see corn-masters sell their whole stock by a few grains of wheat which they carry about with them in a dish, as a sample of the rest, so you by delivering up us, who are but a few, do at the same time unawares surrender up yourselves all together with us;" so we find it related in the history of Aristobulus, the Cassandrian. The Athenians were deliberating, and at a loss what to do, when Demades, having agreed with the persons whom Alexander had demanded, for five talents, undertook to go ambassador, and to intercede with the king for them; and, whether it was that he relied on his friendship and kindness, or that he hoped to find him satiated, as a lion glutted with slaughter, he certainly went, and prevailed with him both to pardon the men, and to be reconciled to the city.

So he and his friends, when Alexander went away, were great men, and Demosthenes was quite put aside. Yet when Agis, the Spartan, made his insurrection, he also for a short time attempted a movement in his favor; but he soon shrunk back again, as the Athenians would not take any part in it, and, Agis being slain, the Lacedæmonians were vanquished. During this time it was that the indictment against Ctesiphon, concerning the crown, was brought to trial. The action was commenced a little before the battle in Chæronea, when Chærondas was archon, but it was not proceeded with till about ten years after, Aristophon being then archon. Never was any public cause more celebrated than this, alike for the fame of the orators, and for the generous courage of the judges, who, though at that time the accusers of Demosthenes were in the height of power, and supported by all the favor of the Macedonians, yet would not give judgment against him, but acquitted him so honorably, that Aeschines did not obtain the fifth part of their suffrages on his side, so that, immediately after, he left the city, and spent the rest of his life in teaching rhetoric about the island of Rhodes, and upon the continent in Ionia.

It was not long after that Harpalus fled from Alexander, and came to Athens out of Asia; knowing himself guilty of many misdeeds into which his love of luxury had led him, and fearing the king, who was now grown terrible even to his best friends. Yet this man had no sooner addressed himself to the people, and delivered up his goods, his ships, and himself to their disposal, but the other orators of the town had their eyes quickly fixed upon his money, and came in to his assistance, persuading the Athenians to receive and protect their suppliant. Demosthenes at first gave advice to chase him out of the country, and to beware lest they involved their city in a war upon an unneccessary and unjust occasion. But some few days after, as they were taking an account of the treasure, Harpalus, perceiving how much he was pleased with a cup of Persian manufacture, and how curiously he surveyed the sculpture and fashion of it, desired him to poise it in his hand, and consider the weight of the gold. Demosthenes, being amazed to feel how heavy it was, asked him what weight it *came to.* "To you," said Harpalus, smiling, "it shall *come with* twenty talents." And presently after, when night drew on, he sent him the cup with so many talents. Harpalus, it seems, was a person of singular skill to discern a man's covetousness by the air of his countenance, and the look and movements of his eyes. For Demosthenes could not resist the temptation, but admitting the present, like an armed garrison, into the citadel of his house, he surrendered himself up to the interest of Harpalus. The next day, he came into the assembly with his neck swathed about with wool and rollers, and when they called on him to rise up and speak, he made signs as if he had lost his voice. But the wits, turning the matter to ridicule, said that certainly the orator had been seized that night with no other than a silver quinsy. And soon after, the people, becoming aware of the bribery, grew angry, and would not suffer him to speak, or make any apology for himself but ran him down with noise; and one man stood

up, and cried out, "What, ye men of Athens, will you not hear
the cup-bearer?" So at length they banished Harpalus out of
the city; and fearing lest they should be called to account for
the treasure which the orators had purloined, they made a
strict inquiry, going from house to house; only Callicles, the son
of Arrhenidas, who was newly married, they would not suffer
to be searched, out of respect, as Theopompus writes, to the
bride, who was within.

Demosthenes resisted the inquisition, and proposed a decree
to refer the business to the court of Areopagus, and to punish
those whom that court should find guilty. But being himself
one of the first whom the court condemned, when he came to
the bar, he was fined fifty talents, and committed to prison;
where, out of shame of the crime for which he was condemned,
and through the weakness of his body, growing incapable of
supporting the confinement, he made his escape, by the care-
lessness of some and by the contrivance of others of the citizens. We are told, at least, that he had not fled far from the city
when, finding that he was pursued by some of those who had
been his adversaries, he endeavored to hide himself. But when
they called him by his name, and coming up nearer to him,
desired he would accept from them some money which they had
brought from home as a provision for his journey, and to that
purpose only had followed him, when they entreated him to
take courage, and to bear up against his misfortune, he burst
out into much greater lamentation, saying, "But how is it possible to support myself under so heavy an affliction, since I leave
a city in which I have such enemies, as in any other it is not
easy to find friends." He did not show much fortitude in his
banishment, spending his time for the most part in Aegina and
Trœzen, and, with tears in his eyes, looking towards the country
of Attica. And there remain upon record some sayings of his,
little resembling those sentiments of generosity and bravery
which he used to express when he had the management of the
commonwealth. For, as he was departing out of the city, it is
reported, he lifted up his hands towards the Acropolis, and
said, "O Lady Minerva, how is it that thou takest delight in
three such fierce untractable beasts, the owl, the snake, and the
people?" The young men that came to visit and converse with

him, he deterred from meddling with state affairs, telling them, that if at first two ways had been proposed to him, the one leading to the speaker's stand and the assembly, the other going direct to destruction, and he could have foreseen the many evils which attend those who deal in public business, such as fears, envies, calumnies, and contentions, he would certainly have taken that which led straight on to his death.

But now happened the death of Alexander, while Demosthenes was in this banishment which we have been speaking of. And the Grecians were once again up in arms, encouraged by the brave attempts of Leosthenes, who was then drawing a circumvallation about Antipater, whom he held close besieged in Lamia. Pytheas, therefore, the orator, and Callimedon, called the Crab, fled from Athens, and taking sides with Antipater, went about with his friends and ambassadors to keep the Grecians from revolting and taking part with the Athenians. But, on the other side, Demosthenes, associating himself with the ambassadors that came from Athens, used his utmost endeavors and gave them his best assistance in persuading the cities to fall unanimously upon the Macedonians, and to drive them out of Greece. Phylarchus says that in Arcadia there happened an encounter between Pytheas and Demosthenes, which came at last to downright railing, while the one pleaded for the Macedonians, and the other for the Grecians. Pytheas said, that as we always suppose there is some disease in the family to which they bring asses' milk, so wherever there comes an embassy from Athens that city must needs be indisposed. And Demosthenes answered him, retorting the comparison: "Asses' milk is brought to restore health and the Athenians come for the safety and recovery of the sick." With this conduct the people of Athens were so well pleased that they decreed the recall of Demosthenes from banishment. The decree was brought in by Demon the Pæanian, cousin to Demosthenes. So they sent him a ship to Aegina, and he landed at the port of Piræus, where he was met and joyfully received by all the citizens, not so much as an archon or a priest staying behind. And Demetrius, the Magnesian, says that he lifted up his hands towards heaven, and blessed this day of his happy return, as far more honorable than that of Alcibiades; since he was recalled by his countrymen, not through any force or constraint put upon them, but by their own good-will and free inclinations. There remained only his pecuniary fine, which, according to law, could not be remitted by the people. But they found out a way to elude the law. It was a custom with them to allow a certain quantity of silver to those who were to furnish and adorn the altar for the sacrifice of Jupiter Soter. This office, for that turn, they bestowed on Demosthenes, and for the performance of it ordered him fifty talents, the very sum in which he was condemned.

Yet it was no long time that he enjoyed his country after his return, the attempts of the Greeks being soon all utterly defeated. For the battle of Cranon happened in Metagitnion, in Boëdromion the garrison entered into Munychia, and in the Pyanepsion following died Demosthenes after this manner.

Upon the report that Antipater and Craterus were coming to Athens, Demosthenes with his party took their opportunity to escape privily out of the city; but sentence of death was, upon the motion of Demades, passed upon them by the people. They dispersed themselves, flying some to one place, some to another; and Antipater sent about his soldiers into all quarters to apprehend them. Archias was their captain, and was thence called the exile-hunter. He was a Thurian born, and is reported to have been an actor of tragedies, and they say that Polus, of Aegina, the best actor of his time, was his scholar; but Hermippus reckons Archias among the disciples of Lacritus, the orator, and Demetrius says he spent some time with Anaximenes. This Archias finding Hyperides the orator, Aritonicus of Marathon, and Himeræus, the brother of Demetrius the Phalerian, in Aegina, took them by force out of the temple of Aecus, whither they were fled for safety, and sent them to Antipater, then at Cleonæ, where they were all put to death; and Hyperides, they say, had his tongue cut out.

Demosthenes, he heard, had taken sanctuary at the temple of Neptune in Calauria and, crossing over thither in some light vessels, as soon as he had landed himself, and the Thracian spearmen that came with him, he endeavored to persuade Demosthenes to accompany him to Antipater, as if he should meet with no hard usage from him. But Demosthenes, in his sleep the night before, had a strange dream. It seemed to him that he was acting a tragedy, and contended with Archias for the victory; and though he acquitted himself well, and gave good satisfaction to the spectators, yet for want of better furniture and provision for the stage, he lost the day. And so, while Archias was discoursing to him with many expressions of kindness, he sat still in the same posture, and looking up steadfastly upon him, "O Archias," said he, "I am as little affected by your promises now as I used formerly to be by your acting." Archias at this beginning to grow angry and to threaten him, "Now," said Demosthenes, "you speak like the genuine Macedonian oracle; before you were but acting a part. Therefore forbear only a little, while I write a word or two home to my family." Having thus spoken, he withdrew into the temple and taking a scroll as if he meant to write, he put the reed into his mouth, and biting it as he was wont to do when he was thoughtful or writing, he held it there some time. Then he bowed down his head and covered it. The soldiers that stood at the door, supposing all this to proceed from want of courage and fear of death, in derision called him effeminate, and faint-hearted, and coward. And Archias drawing near, desired him to rise up, and repeating the same kind of thing he had spoken before, he once more promised to make his peace with Antipater. But Demosthenes, perceiving that now the poison had pierced, and seized his vitals, uncovered his head, and fixing his eyes upon Archias, "Now," said he, "as soon as you please, you may commence the part of Creon in the tragedy, and cast out this body of mine unburied. But, O gracious Neptune, I, for my part while I am yet alive will rise up and depart out of this sacred place; though Antipater and the Macedonians have not left so much as thy temple unpolluted." After he had thus spoken and desired to be held up, because already he began to tremble and stagger, as he was going forward, and passing by the altar, he fell down, and with a groan gave up the ghost.

Ariston says that he took the poison out of a reed, as we have shown before. But Pappus, a certain historian whose history was recovered by Hermippus, says, that as he fell near the altar, there was found in his scroll this beginning only of a letter, and nothing more, "Demosthenes to Antipater." And that when his sudden death was much wondered at, the Thracians who guarded the doors reported that he took the poison into his hand out of a rag, and put it in his mouth, and that they imagined it had been gold which he swallowed, but the maid that served him, being examined by the followers of Archias, affirmed that he had worn it in a bracelet for a long time, as an amulet. And Eratosthenes also says that he kept the poison in a hollow ring, and that that ring was the bracelet which he wore about his arm. There are various other statements made by the many authors who have related the story, but there is no need to enter into their discrepancies; yet I must not omit what is said by Demochares the relation of Demosthenes, who is of opinion it was not by the help of poison that he met with so sudden and so easy a death, but that by the singular favor and providence of the gods he was thus rescued from the cruelty of the Macedonians. He died on the sixteenth of Pyanepsion, the most sad and solemn day of the Thesmophoria, which the women observe by fasting in the temple of the goddess.

Soon after his death, the people of Athens bestowed on him such honors as he had deserved. They erected his statue of brass; they decreed that the eldest of his family should be maintained in the Prytaneum; and on the base of his statue was engraven the famous inscription—

> "Had you for Greece been strong, as wise you were,
> The Macedonian had not conquered her."

For it is simply ridiculous to say, as some have related, that Demosthenes made these verses himself in Calauria, as he was about to take the poison.

A little before he went to Athens, the following incident was said to have happened. A soldier, being summoned to appear before his superior officer, and answer to an accusation brought against him, put that little gold which he had into the hands of Demosthenes's statue. The fingers of this statue were folded one within another, and near it grew a small plane-tree, from which many leaves, either accidently blown thither by the wind, or placed so on purpose by the man himself, falling together and lying round about the gold, concealed it for a long time. In the end, the soldier returned and found his treasure entire, and the fame of this incident was spread abroad. And many ingenious persons of the city competed with each other, on this occasion, to vindicate the integrity of Demosthenes in several epigrams which they made on the subject.

As for Demades, he did not long enjoy the new honors he now came in for, divine vengeance for the death of Demosthenes pursuing him into Macedonia, where he was justly put to death by those whom he had basely flattered. They were weary of him before, but at this time the guilt he lay under was manifest and undeniable. For some of his letters were intercepted, in which he had encouraged Perdiccas to fall upon Macedonia, and to save the Grecians, who, he said, hung only by an old rotten thread, meaning Antipater. Of this he was accused by Dinarchus, the Corinthian, and Cassander was so enraged, that he first slew his son in his bosom, and then gave orders to execute him; who might now at last, by his own extreme misfortunes, learn the lesson that traitors who made sale of their country sell themselves first; a truth which Demosthenes had often foretold him, and he would never believe. Thus, Sosius, you have the life of Demosthenes from such accounts as we have either read or heard concerning him.

The Oratorical Career of Demosthenes

by George Kennedy

The antithesis of Isocrates as an educator is Plato, as an orator Demosthenes. This is true not only in the specific historical sense that Demosthenes' energies were directed against Macedon but in the attitude of the two orators toward speech and policy. To Isocrates oratory is a thing in itself; artistic creativity is his goal; he looks for what is literarily expedient. Demosthenes, though he begins as a rhetorician and logographer,* subdues his art and constrains it to be his tool in the defense of his country. Once his political instincts are fully awakened they establish absolute standards: he can be inconsistent about all things except patriotism, and to that end his oratory is the single greatest means.

There is a very weak tradition (Plutarch, *Lives of the Ten Orators* 844b) that makes Demosthenes a pupil of Isocrates, and attempts have been made to point out specific influences of

* In this period, a logographer was a writer of speeches for other men to deliver. [Editor's note.]

one on the other.[1] But Demosthenes' whole concept of the function of the orator, of art, of style, and of politics is so essentially different that occasional verbal similarities need only mean that Demosthenes had read and occasionally picked up a phrase from Isocrates. We have said before that he may have studied some kind of judicial handbook circulated in Isocrates' school, for he was to a great extent self-taught.[2] When he was still a boy the oratory of Callistratus first roused in him a desire to be a great speaker (Plutarch, *Demosthenes* 5). He definitely learned something from Isaeus when preparing his prosecution of his guardians,[3] and the story (Plutarch, *Demosthenes* 7) that his delivery was criticized and improved by the actor Satyrus may well be true. Although they have not always admired him, all critics, ancient and modern, have felt the uniqueness of Demosthenes: it is seen in his Periclean isolation, his disinterest in the gymnasium, his water-drinking among the wine bibbers, his autodidacticism, his ability to draw something from everyone.

In the oratorical career of Demosthenes certain speeches illustrate critical steps in his development. The following discussion will deal with them in an attempt to outline the most satisfactory critical approach to his rhetoric. Any greater discussion covering all the speeches would be out of proportion to this work.

Demosthenes' earliest speech, his prosecution of his guardian Aphobus, is a remarkable product, as much a piece of accounting as of rhetoric.[4] Despite the attested influence of

---

[1] Avoidance of hiatus, a favorite stylistic feature of Isocrates, can be seen in Demosthenes, and some of the verbalization of patriotism in Demosthenes may come from Isocrates; cf. Josef Mesk, "Demosthenes und Isokrates," *Wiener Studien*, 23 (1901), 209 ff.; Paul Wendland, "Isokrates und Demosthenes," *Nachrichten von der Gesellschaft der Wissenschaft zu Göttingen* (1910), 289 ff.; Werner Jaeger, *Demosthenes: The Origin and Growth of His Policy* (Berkeley: University of California Press, 1938), pp. 31 ff.

[2] Cf. Jaeger, pp. 31 f.

[3] Cf. Friedrich Blass, *Die attische Beredsamkeit*, 3 vols. (Leipzig, 1874–93), 3.i.14 ff. and 199 ff. and Octave Navarre, introduction to the Budé *Démosthène: plaidoyers politiques* (Paris, 1954), Vol. 1, pp. xxx f.

[4] Cf. Blass, 3.1.199 ff.; Jaeger, p. 244; Walther Schwahn, *Demosthenes gegen Aphobos: ein Beitrag zur Geschichte der griechischen Wirtschaft* (Leipzig, 1929), tried to work out the financial details but was not en-

Isaeus, the character of the speech is much more open than is usual in Isaeus. The direct evidence is relevant and extensive: statement and substantiation, statement and substantiation, again and again. Argument from probability finds only a limited use (e.g. section 55). There is no indulgence of love of speech, no unnecessary word. The shamelessness of Aphobus is shown repeatedly (e.g. 38), but there is no scurrility. Though the speech falls into the standard formal parts: prooemium 1–3 (with the usual attack on the intractability of the opponent, expression of inexperience—justified for once—and request for a fair hearing), narrative 4–6, proof 7–48 (with 47–48 as a recapitulation), refutation 49–59, and peroration 60–69 (with indirect recapitulation and effective pathos), the impression of the speech is entirely narrative, as though the orator were telling his story and proving every word. Except for the increase in pathos at the end the parts do not show the stylistic differences found in parts of other such speeches. Nothing is probably more reassuring and convincing to a jury than this candid technique. An orator can only use it if he has a very good case with many documents and witnesses and is himself the complete master of the material.

The second speech against Aphobus is a reply in the same trial to Aphobus' charge that Demosthenes' father was a public debtor. It is less successful, less thought out. Direct evidence was not procurable, for the attack had come unexpectedly, and Demosthenes apparently delivered the first part of the speech extempore.[5] There is no formal narration, which is not unusual in "second" speeches; however, one is really needed here to explain the basis of the charge, and the orator fills up the void with a representation of facts from the first speech and a proportionally larger peroration, perhaps to be expected since this is the conclusion of his case. The speech is not a poor one. De-

---

tirely successful; cf. the review by George M. Calhoun, *Classical Philology*, 25 (1930), 86 ff. Cf. also J. Korver, "Demosthenes gegen Aphobos," *Mnemosyne*, 10 (1941), 8 ff.

[5] Cf. Alfred P. Dorjahn, "A Third Study of Demosthenes' Ability to Speak Extemporaneously," *Transactions of the American Philological Association*, 83 (1952), 164 ff. Dorjahn has shown in this and other studies that there is no good evidence for the tradition that Demosthenes was unable to speak extemporaneously.

mosthenes did what he could at the time, he does not allow himself to be led into any wild statements, and the impression of the case which the jury had from the first speech was doubtless confirmed.

The third speech against Aphobus was delivered some time later, after Aphobus had brought a suit of false witness against Phanus, who had testified for Demosthenes.[6] It was necessary to discuss the earlier trial, and the nature of the attack meant that little direct evidence was available; thus, the use of argument from probability (e.g. 22 ff.) makes the speech seem more regular than the two earlier works, though at the end of the narration (10) the speaker makes a distinction between probabilities and argument from what seems just to all. The speech has great versatility not only in argument but also in style, for example in the liveliness of the imaginary debate between Demosthenes and Aphobus in 40–41. The speech ends abruptly, but perhaps the peroration was not published or has been lost.

Although Demosthenes continued to have difficulties with his guardians and soon afterward delivered the first and second speeches *Against Onetor,* it must have been the prosecution of Aphobus which gave him a limited fame as a writer of courtroom speeches. For the rest of his life he was a logographer; we cannot say with what frequency since many of the works he wrote probably were not preserved or published. His clients seem to have been carefully chosen from among friends and equals: he was not the defender of the downtrodden, but of the affluent, of the creditor against the debtor. Birth was not important to him, as his defense of Phormio shows, but money was. Even when his clients claim poverty one finds it difficult to believe them. In the speech *Against Callicles* the client says that he has small means, but he does not care about the money (35) and has recently paid something over a thousand drachmae in fines (2). Of all the clients the most modest in circumstances was perhaps Euxitheus, who prosecutes Eubulides in the fifty-seventh oration. His opponents claimed that he was

---

[6] Cf. George M. Calhoun, "A Problem of Authenticity (Demosthenes 29)," *Transactions of the American Philological Association,* 65 (1934), 80 ff.

rich, but he denies this (52) and there are indications of poverty in the speech (25 and 31). If Euxitheus was indeed poor, it is tempting to see a political significance in Demosthenes' acceptance of the case, for the speech was delivered in the mid 340's during the great campaign against Philip, when Demosthenes wanted to arouse popular sentiment.

The surviving private orations of Demosthenes show him to be a business-like logographer. He can portray the character of a client with conviction, he can narrate with clarity and vigor, and he can construct a logical proof without an impression of slyness. He usually follows standard rhetorical structure and employs many of the commonplaces of proemium, proof, and peroration.* But for all Demosthenes' technical skill there is virtually no evidence in the private speeches of that point of view, seen in Lysias, Isaeus, and Isocrates, which regarded rhetoric as a joy in itself. Demosthenes accepted cases, it would seem, not to find occasions to prove his cleverness, but to gratify his friends and make money. He did not seek sensationalism, did not deal with adulterers and courtesans, did not introduce spectacular pathetic effects.

There is perhaps only one instance in which a charge of questionable practice could be brought against Demosthenes. In the thirty-sixth speech he ably defended the banker Phormio in a suit brought by Apollodorus for recovery of twenty talents. Phormio had been an employee of Apollodorus' father, and after the latter's death became the trustee of his estate. Releases were given for all claims, but after many years had passed Apollodorus again insisted that money was owed to him. Phormio, with Demosthenes' speech, won more than four-fifths of the jurors' votes and Apollodorus had to pay a fine. Soon afterward Apollodorus brought suit for false witness against a minor witness in Phormio's defense, one Stephanus. We have a speech (45) apparently written by Demosthenes on behalf of Apollodorus which contains a virulent attack on Phormio (71 ff.). The orator's change of clients has been much discussed. Was he simply available to the higher bidder without himself feeling any involvement in the cases? This would

* In modern terms, the introduction, supporting materials, and conclusion of a speech. [Editor's note.]

seem more probable in the case of other orators than Demosthenes, who apparently picked his clients with care. Aeschines (*On the Embassy* 328) criticizes Demosthenes for showing the speech for Phormio to Apollodorus before the trial, not for writing a speech for him. Several hundred years later Plutarch criticized the action and regarded it as clearly morally wrong, but Plutarch may not have understood the conventional standards of logography. Blass suggested and others have agreed that Demosthenes' change of sides was influenced by political consideration, since Apollodorus took the personal risk about this time of proposing transference of the theoric fund to the war chest (*Against Neaera* 4), a motion consistent with Demosthenes' recommendations in the *Olynthiacs*.[7] A political trade of this kind is probably no more admirable than a lack of involvement and purely literary attitude toward a client's case, but it does show that Demosthenes' actions were based on what he thought to be patriotic principles. The personal attack on Phormio is, however, an acceptance of rhetorical convention, maybe insisted upon by Apollodorus, but regrettable.

Among the private orations is one (51) which does not belong to that category, a claim for a trierarchic crown, delivered some time after 361 by a speaker who was supported by Cephisodotus. We know that Demosthenes as a trierarch carried Cephisodotus as general on board his ship to the Chersonese in 360/359 (Aeschines, *Against Ctesiphon* 51 f.), an occasion vividly described by Demosthenes later (*Against Aristocrates* 163 ff.). The facts fit well enough to make it probable that Demosthenes is speaking in his own person and the speech is, therefore, evidence that he was wealthy enough to be required to furnish a warship at this time, not indeed the only occasion on which he did so (*Against Midias* 78 and 161). It is also evidence of a difference of opinion between Demosthenes and certain supporters of Aristophon (16), then the first man in the city. The speech is not impressive rhetorically; it is querulous in tone and has none of the breadth of vision which Demosthenes

[7] Blass, 3.1.32 ff. and Jaeger, p. 40. J. E. Sandys and F. A. Paley, *Select Private Orations of Demosthenes* (Cambridge, Eng., 1896), Vol. 2, pp. xxxix ff. discuss the matter thoroughly, but do not accept Blass' view. On the portrait of the disputants cf. Ivo Bruns, *Das literarische Portrat der Griechen* (Berlin, 1896), pp. 534 ff.

later develops: no mention is made, for example, of what the ships did or were intended to do.

As a result of his success in private cases (*dikai*) Demosthenes gained an opportunity to write speeches in suits involving an offense against the state (*graphai*), where there was usually an underlying political rivalry. Greater public interest was aroused by these, and the speeches are often two or three times as long as speeches in private cases. Since Athens had no public prosecutor, individuals had to bring charges in the public suits, and the actual speeches delivered might be written for the prosecutors by logographers, just as in private suits. Demosthenes' function has not changed, therefore, in his speeches *Against Androtion* (355), *Against Timocrates* (353), and *Against Aristocrates* (352), but opportunity for imaginative treatment and fame are much greater. The speech *Against Leptines* (355) is not essentially different from the private speeches, though Plutarch (*Demosthenes* 15) reports that Demosthenes spoke it in public himself, which would be a further step toward an active public career. Nor has Demosthenes' economic view altered. *Against Androtion, Against Timocrates,* and *Against Leptines* are all directed against a taxation policy that had been especially hard on Demosthenes' prosperous friends and clients.[8] All these works may be regarded as support for the conservative, peace-minded Eubulus. This does not, of course, mean that Demosthenes' views are in any way oligarchic.[9] Eubulus was not an oligarch nor was his supporter

---

[8] Cf. L. Vorndran, *Die Aristocratea des Demosthenes als Advokatensrede und ihre politische Tendenz* (Paderborn, 1922) and Jaeger, pp. 56 ff. The difficulties of associating terms descriptive of policy to the basically personal groupings of Athenian politics are well brought out by Raphael Sealey, "Athens after the Social War," *Journal of Hellenistic Studies*, 75 (1955), 74 ff. Sealey discusses the political circumstances of the three speeches in question and prefers to regard Aristophon and Androtion as members of two groups personally opposed, but promoting the same policies.

[9] Pierre Orsini, in the introduction to the Budé *Démosthène: plaidoyers politiques* (Paris, 1954), Vol. 1, pp. ix ff., desiring to make Demosthenes a democrat, has wrongly tried to deny that he was a defender of wealth and position. Orsini's hero worship of Demosthenes' wisdom is counterbalanced in the second part of the introduction where Octave Navarre, the co-editor, writing a number of years earlier, discusses Demosthenes' technique in these speeches.

Aeschines, nor, in fact, was oligarchy an important ideology in fourth-century Athenian politics. The democratic sentiments of Demosthenes' early speeches can be quite sincere and yet his sympathies can be with the wealthy. The Athenian system of relying on the rich for large capital expenses meant that the state's finances were only as sound as the finances of wealthy individuals. Demosthenes' bias for wealth was to him a bias in favor of financial order.

Since the speeches are consistent in function and social viewpoint with what Demosthenes had been doing, it seems appropriate to ask whether there is any rhetorical difference between these speeches and the private orations, taking *Against Androtion* and *Against Leptines* as examples.

In the public orations of Demosthenes it is often necessary to distinguish the object of a speech from its subject, or, to put it another way, the real from the ostensible and legal issue. The real objective of the speech against Androtion is to discredit a political faction which had been hard upon the wealthier class of society. Androtion as a tax gatherer had especially won the ill will of many. We do not know whether his motives were patriotic or demagogic. An excuse for prosecuting him was found in his proposal to crown the members of the outgoing council, a traditional mark of honor, although in this year (356/355) they had not fulfilled the technical requirement of building new ships because the treasurer had absconded with the money. The charge of illegality was, in other words, a legal technicality. The two prosecutors, coming from the same humble class as the jury, were personal enemies of Androtion, which was satisfactory since personal enmity was a tolerable ground for litigation in Athens and could effectively mask more complicated motives. We do not know who wrote the first speech for the prosecution, perhaps Euctemon, who delivered it. Demosthenes composed the second speech, delivered by Diodorus.

The rhetorical problem involved was to make the action of Androtion seem sufficiently grave to justify condemnation. Demosthenes had to convert a legal technicality into a threat to Athens. He no doubt believed in his cause, and he was aided by Androtion's arbitrary methods and the fact that, as a former pupil of Isocrates (Anonymous life of Isocrates, line 104, Budé), he could be presented as a tricky sophist. Demosthenes' chief technique, and the striking feature of the speech, is the interweaving of three themes: Androtion is vicious, Androtion's crimes are a public concern, Androtion is a sophist. There is a systematic generalization of the charge, or elevation of it from the immediate and legalistic to the symbolic and patriotic. These techniques, first used here, became permanent features of Demosthenes' art.

The three themes are stated in the proemium (1–4). Androtion has done dreadful things to Euctemon, but worse things to Diodorus. Worse than that, he has attacked Diodorus' uncle. Worse than that, he now has harmed the entire state. But the judges must be careful and not misled, for Androtion is a clever sophist. The themes are rhetorical commonplaces, but usually they are restricted to the prooemium. The distinctive feature of Demosthenes' treatment is that throughout the systematic discussion that follows these threads are never dropped; perhaps the first is the most prominent, but the others continually appear.

The generalization of the charge begins with the first words of the speech, where Euctemon is said to have come to the aid of the city as well as of himself. Androtion's assertion that the council was not responsible for the loss of the funds and its consequent inability to build ships presents an opportunity for amplification of the importance of the navy (12 ff.) with examples from Persian, Peloponnesian, and fourth-century wars, all leaving the clear impression that Androtion is undermining national defense. Androtion must be convicted as a warning to future councils that they must build ships to be honored (19–20). The charge that Androtion was technically incompetent to take part in the assembly is likewise made the occasion for amplification of the wisdom of Solon in guarding Athens against immoral leaders (31–32). Gradually Demosthenes builds up a picture of Androtion as a would-be oligarch: his conviction will make the council more democratic and Athens a better place (37). Are the constitution, the laws, the oaths of the jurymen to be bartered away for the small amount of overdue taxes collected by the plaintiff (45)? The methods of An-

drotion are oligarchic and exceed the violence of the Thirty
Tyrants (47 ff.). The citizens are in fact being treated as slaves
(55). Thus Androtion becomes a symbol: whatever kind of
man is honored in the state will be imitated (64); the golden
crowns which he destroyed are a symbol of merit and honor,
qualities held highest by Athenians (75); the bowls dedicated
by Androtion are only symbols of wealth. What impiety for
Androtion to be conducting the sacred rites of Athens (78)!

By the time Demosthenes has finished speaking Androtion
seems a monster and the charge a crucial one in the preservation of the state. The problem of social prejudice is cleverly
avoided by granting that rich men were wrong to fail to pay
their taxes (42) and subsequently speaking as though Androtion were mainly exacting taxes from the poor (65). Demosthenes has likewise avoided attacking the council members of
the past year and asserts that no disgrace will be brought upon
them by condemning the actions of these few culprits (36).
The speech was heard but once, and in once hearing or once
reading today the logical fallacies and exaggerations are not
easily perceived. It is possible that some of the facts were more
adequately dealt with in the speech given by Euctemon. Demosthenes does not *prove* that the methods of Androtion were
oligarchic, nor that he had been a prostitute, nor that his father
had been a state debtor—a charge which had been used
against Demosthenes himself by Aphobus—certainly not that
he had defrauded the treasury as is implied toward the end of
the speech (76). It is highly unlikely that Androtion's methods
were worse than those of the Thirty Tyrants: Demosthenes
produces nothing to equal the experience of Lysias and his
family. Demosthenes objects to the use of alternative defenses
by Androtion (18) but introduces alternatives himself later on
(e.g. 37 and 44). He is also unfair in denying the right of a
defendant to dispute the method by which he is brought to
trial (28). In other words, there are sophisms and tricks to be
found and Demosthenes is clearly a rhetorician. But his motives, unlike those of Lysias, Isocrates, and Isaeus, are not rhetorical, they are political or economic. The end, the discrediting
of Androtion, is what is really important and personally important to Demosthenes, though he does not personally deliver the

speech. If unfair and tricky, he is yet personally consistent and sincere.

The speech *Against Androtion* has regularity of form and clear structural members. There is a prooemium (1–4) dealing with plaintiff, defendant, motive, and significance as usual. A narration is strictly unnecessary, since this is a second speech for the prosecution; but sections five through seven function as a narration in making a statement of the case, and the usual word introducing the narration (γάρ) is found. The proof extends from section eight to sixty-eight. It is divided into a demonstration, with enthymemes and examples, of the illegality of Androtion's action (8–20), of his immorality (21–24), of the legality of the prosecution (25–34), then a refutation of the points made by Androtion (35–46) and an attack on Androtion's character (47–68). The peroration is introduced as though it was a further discussion of the faults and errors of the defendant. There is no recapitulation, but the pathos increases in the presentation of the crowns and bowls as symbols and in the introduction of the religious motif at the very end.[10]

Against Leptines is part of the same political program and is an attempt to repeal a law invalidating grants of immunities to the ordinary recurring liturgies or financial burdens imposed upon the rich. Some wealthy citizens, Chabrias for example, had at one time been exempted because of unusual services to the state. Leptines had abolished the exemptions ostensibly to equalize the financial burden on other citizens. Demosthenes is no doubt sincere in believing that these honorable grants served an important function in encouraging public responsibility, but it is nevertheless true that the class with which he has been identified benefited most from the immunities. The speech contains (24–25) a spirited defense of the existence of private wealth in the state in which Demosthenes' viewpoint is

[10] Navarre, *op. cit.*, supra n. 111, pp. xxx ff., has a very different notion of the structure of the speech, as does William Wayte, *Demosthenes' Against Androtion and Against Timocrates* (Cambridge, Eng., 1893), pp. xxvi ff., but they do not recognize that introductory words betray the vestiges of a "normal" structure and that ethos, invective, and pathos can be regarded as forms of proof—are so regarded by Aristotle. There is no necessity to restrict the contents of the *pistis* to rational argument. The term epilogue, applied by Navarre (pp. xxvi ff.) to the better part of the speech, is exceedingly inappropriate for such use.

clearly seen. Furthermore, the law of Leptines abolishing the immunities was clearly a part of the same political program as Androtion's tax gathering activities. Aristophon, the statesman in power at the time, was one of the commissioners defending the changes made by Leptines (148), and Eubulus, the leader of the opposite group and soon to become the leading Athenian statesman, was one of those who had been granted an immunity (137). According to Plutarch (*Demosthenes* 15) Demosthenes spoke in person, perhaps in hopes of marrying the widow of Chabrias, whose son, deprived of his father's immunity, nominally was bringing the charge against the new law. The speech is unique in being a prosecution of a law rather than an individual. Since the statute of limitations prevented prosecution of Leptines himself, Demosthenes attacked his law instead and proposed a substitute for it. Commissioners were appointed to defend Leptines' law.

If Demosthenes did speak in person we can see his image in the ethos of the speech. Jaeger drew a picture of a restrained, dignified, somewhat aristocratic advisor—in a word a humanist.[11] Critics have admired the polished tone and assured elegance of the speech, but its conservatism is equally striking. The laws and constitution are viewed as a political framework evolved with care throughout the past, unexcelled in wisdom. Change is most to be distrusted. What has made Athens great once will do so again (e.g. 88 ff.).

The rhetorical problem of *Against Leptines* is a simpler one than in the case of *Against Androtion*. Obviously the matter is not just a technicality; the speaker must show that the benefits of granting immunities more than balance the immediate financial advantages of abolishing immunities. His theme invites a wide discussion of national self-interest and public service. This is the earliest speech in which Demosthenes begins to formulate his vision of a national character, and he uses that actual phrase a couple of times (11 and 64). He also (61) views Philip of Macedon with some alarm.

Rhetorically the most interesting feature of the speech is its structure. This at first appears in the extreme, merely a series of points strung together and introduced by an almost

[11] Jaeger, pp. 65 ff.

unvarying τοίνυν, "well then." Such a technique contributed
to the ethos of the speaker, who seems no slick and ranting
professional, but a respectable citizen saying what he has to
say. On closer inspection, however, the structure turns out to
be somewhat more complex. Demosthenes' proposal for a substitute law is set in the very center of the speech (88–104)
and framed by two attacks upon the law of Leptines, each divided into two parts. Thus, after a very brief prooemium (1)
there comes first (2–28) the general objections against Leptines' law based on the topics of justice, expediency, honor,
profit—the typical topics of fourth-century deliberative oratory
—rather artlessly woven together. Then follows (29–35) a section devoted to historical examples of those who deserved and
received immunities, what Blass called the "positive" side of
the case.[12] Such examples are relevant to the issue, unlike those
introduced by Isocrates in the *Philip*. After the discussion of
the substitute law comes the negative side of the case, the refutation of claims made in support of Leptines' law (105–133),
and finally a section which returns to the general considerations
of the beginning: justice, honor, and expediency (134–156).
The speech ends with a not unemotional peroration of recapitulation. A modern Belgian school of critics has stressed Demosthenes' use in many speeches of a "psychological" structure
rather than the traditional rhetorical arrangement;[13] certainly it
can be agreed that he shows no signs of being the docile fol-
lower of rhetorical rules. He carries along simultaneously a
number of different themes, all of which are repeatedly illus-
trated and each of which is repeatedly brought to the surface.
The symmetry which the speech contains may seem rather artificial, but Demosthenes' artistic independence and ability to
synthesize standard topics into a whole which will effect a

---

[12] Blass, 3.1.235.
[13] Cf. Marcel Delaunois, "Du plan logique au plan psychologique chez
Démosthène," *Les Etudes classiques*, 19 (1951), 177 ff., "Le plan rhé-
torique dans l'éloquence grecque d'Homère à Démosthène," *Les Etudes
classiques*, 23 (1955), 267 ff., and an amplification of the subject under
the latter title, Brussels, 1959. Cf. also H. de Raedt, "Plan psychologique
de la première *Philippique* de Démosthène," *Les Etudes classiques*, 19
(1952), 227 ff. These studies show on graphs the interweaving of motifs
in Demosthenes.

practical end, and not simply stand as a monument of words, are already evident.

In 354 Demosthenes delivered his earliest surviving deliberative speech, *On the Symmories*. It is much more compressed than any of the works we have been discussing, too compressed, perhaps, for oral presentation; therefore, we may well have a revision of what was actually said. The topics are more systematically treated than in *Against Leptines*, but the structure is again symmetrical: after a brief prooemium attacking impractical orators Demosthenes deals first with the proposed Persian war, which he opposes (3–13); expediency (3), honor (6), justice (7), and possibility (9) are the topics touched upon. This takes us about a third of the way through the speech. At the center is the discussion of ways and means for war: Demosthenes does not oppose preparations, but money must be allowed to remain in the hands of its owners (24 ff.), a course which is possible, honorable, and expedient. Roughly the last third of the speech is devoted to a refutation of the need to fight Persia, a peroration emphasizing justice, and the concluding, matter-of-fact recapitulation. This topical approach can also be seen in the early speech *On the Liberty of the Rhodians* (351): practicality, expediency, and honor all point in one direction (2, 8, and 28).

About this time two changes take place in Demosthenes' work. One is political. After supporting the program of Eubulus, which was based on financial security at home and peace abroad, Demosthenes rather suddenly turns against Eubulus in alarm at the continued growth of the power of Philip. The change can be attributed largely to Philip's unexpected successes in Thessaly and Thrace.[14] The first fruit of the new point of view is the first *Philippic*.[15] Since such a change must have alienated many of Demosthenes' friends he could only have

---

[14] Cf. Jaeger, p. 114.

[15] The dates of the speech *On the Liberty of the Rhodians* and the first *Philippic* are in doubt. Jaeger seems right, p. 230, n. 41, in regarding the Rhodian speech as similar to that *On the Symmories* and *For the Megalopolitans*, but "still far removed from the impassioned national feeling of the Philippics" (94). A good discussion of Desmosthenic chronology is Raphael Sealey, "Dionysius of Halicarnassus and Some Demosthenic Dates," *Revue des études grecques*, 68 (1955), 77 ff.

had a sincere and patriotic belief that a determined opposition to Philip was best for Athens. The personal concerns of Demosthenes' wealthy associates are swept aside as trivial.

Corresponding to this political change is a rhetorical change. New vigor appears in the first *Philippic*, unlike anything in Greek oratory since the sharply focused speeches in Thucydides. There is no question of weighing the relative expediency of courses of action and of attributing to them justice and honor. It is assumed that Philip acts in his own interest, and Athens must act in hers. Territory in the north is the prize of war. The property of the careless belongs to those willing to run a risk (5). Demosthenes so focuses Athenian interests that the question seems not one of advantage, but of necessity, not the choice of a course of action, but the pursuit of the only possibility. His major point is that success is possible (2–12). All other rhetorical arguments are only accessory: Athens' failure to act will bring on her the deepest disgrace and will allow Philip to go unpunished (42–43), but no honor is promised Athens for action, and disinterested justice is not involved. It seems that Demosthenes' patience has been suddenly exhausted; the futility of expecting right to triumph in the course of nature has overwhelmed him.[16]

Succeeding speeches show a similar intensity. The first *Olynthiac*, for example, makes no mention of the honor or justice to be observed in helping Olynthus, only of the fact that it is to Athens' interest to seize the opportunity presented to fight Philip near his own home (11). Finally, in the second and third *Philippics* Demosthenes takes a further step. His idea of expediency had never been that of the speakers in Thucydides. Perhaps expedient policy was not so evident in the bewildering fourth century as it had been a hundred years before. The ugly principle that might makes right was no longer acceptable: the fourth century demanded at least an appearance of justice, morality, and rectitude, which is no doubt at the bottom of the common synthesis of topics. Beginning with the second *Philippic* Demosthenes finds a basis for his argumentation in a higher

[16] George A. Kennedy, "Focusing of Arguments in Greek Deliberative Oratory," *Transactions of the American Philological Association*, 90 (1959), 131 ff.

principle than self-interest, and one which combines ethical nobility with rhetorical force. This is the concept of the national character. Philip looks only to the immediately expedient, and most other Greek states are as bad, Demosthenes says, but Athens has the tradition of her past to demand her loyalty (7–10). Self-interest and expediency for her are thus primarily the maintenance of this tradition. The third *Philippic,* Demosthenes' most forceful speech, carries on this same spirit. Justice in the old sense is not discussed and expediency is coupled with the possibility of preserving Athens (4). There are none of the self-conscious topics of the professional rhetoricians, yet the whole speech is concerned with the necessity of action in Athens' interest. Failure to act will inevitably bring disgrace for all that Athens has been, and the orator's vision of the national character is the point on which the whole speech focuses and under which all arguments are subsumed. It is also the physical center of the speech (36 ff.) framed symmetrically by considerations of practical concerns of the moment. A battle for Athens, decadent and fond of flattery, forgetful of her past, is fought out between Demosthenes the unpopular patriot (2) and Philip, the violent foreign king, compared successively to a fever (29) and a hailstorm (33).

Surely this viewpoint, like Demosthenes' political position, is one of stubborn, unselfcentered patriotism. The normal goals of the rhetorician and politician are equally rejected for the faith of the prophet. There appears to have been an austerity and loftiness in Demosthenes even in his early career; perhaps this finds expression in his deliberate self-devotion to a cause which, it must have been increasingly clear, was impossible. A splendid passage of *On the Crown* (190 ff.) betrays the instinct of the martyr. It must be read with recognition of Demosthenes' assumption that no fundamental change could be admitted into the Athenian constitution and traditional way of life, an assumption which others did not accept and which could not permanently be maintained. In his lonely radicalism, Demosthenes was a pure conservative.

Patriotism, to one who does not share an enthusiasm for a particular cause, can be very distressing, for the patriot is capable of ignoring details of specific and inconvenient facts, social

conventions, or even ordinary responsibility. The more he believes in his goal, the more it seems to justify all means of at-
tainment. His cloak is his sincerity and his shield the fact that
he defends others who cannot or will not defend themselves;
but his position can become absurd. In responding to a purely
rhetorical challenge the rhetorician, perhaps with tongue in
cheek, colors and molds his case within the limits of probability;
the patriot, in pursuit of what seems essential, is occasionally
blinded to probability. The unattractive aspect of Demosthenes'
oratory is mostly the result of the purity of his patriotism; it can
best be seen in the prosecutions which arose from the Peace of
Philocrates.

After the fall of Olynthus Demosthenes apparently became
convinced that at least a temporary truce with Macedon was
necessary, because Athens was not making any progress in the
war. Negotiations were conducted in 346 and Demosthenes
took part, together with Philocrates, Aeschines, and others.
Aeschines describes (*On the Embassy* 21 ff.) Demosthenes'
conduct during the trip to see Philip: he had promised foun-
tains of words and boasted that he would sew up Philip's
mouth with an unsoaked rush. His speech was to be the climax
of the interview, but, when the moment came, Demosthenes
collapsed completely. He fumbled his prooemium and finally
stopped, helpless. Philip, Aeschines relates, was rather conde-
scending and encouraged Demosthenes, but that just aggra-
vated the orator. Finally the herald imperiously commanded
the withdrawal of the ambassadors. Various inferences can be
drawn from the story; one is that Demosthenes did not have the
instinct for replying to a sudden rhetorical challenge, which
Aeschines shows; another is that his collapse represents his
painful horror at speaking, more or less as an inferior, before a
barbarian; in other words, it was a result of the greatness of his
love of Athens. It may well also be true that this incident is the
source of his great hatred of Aeschines, who claims to have
distinguished himself oratorically, perhaps for the very reason
that he was less emotionally involved in the situation. It was to
Aeschines that Philip addressed his reply.

The peace was achieved, though Philip dallied and secured
more territory before swearing to it. Contrary to Athenian ex-

pectations, which had been encouraged by Aeschines, Philip
then advanced into central Greece and reduced the cities of
Phocis, which he had prevented from being expressly included
in the treaty. Inevitably those responsible for the peace found
themselves attacked. Demosthenes, no doubt anxious to show
that he had played no active role in making the peace (*On the
False Embassy* 223), turned his guns on Aeschines. But he
showed the irresponsibility of the frenzied patriot in so doing,
for the hatchet man he chose to oppose the hated Aeschines
was one Timarchus, a man long active against Philip (*On the
False Embassy* 286), but whose private life was notorious. Aeschines immediately charged that Timarchus' crimes made it illegal for him to participate in public deliberations and to bring
actions. Aeschines prevailed, but Demosthenes remembered.

Three years later, encouraged by Hyperides' successful
prosecution of Philocrates, Demosthenes personally pressed the
prosecution of Aeschines. The speech, known as *On the False
Embassy*, attempts to achieve on a very large scale (three hundred and three sections) the passion of the *Philippics*, the clarity of Demosthenes' earlier prosecutions, and the subtlety of
interwoven themes, especially the vision of Athenian national
character, which underlies all of Demosthenes' work. All in all
the speech is a failure. Despite some fine bursts of rhetoric, it is
unpersuasive and misleading. Demosthenes is most interested
in an opportunity to discredit Aeschines generally. As in the
prosecution of Androtion he wishes to amplify a charge into a
sweeping denunciation, though here the specific indictment is
no legal technicality, but the grave accusation of receiving
bribes from Philip. This Demosthenes does not come near to
proving: there was in fact no evidence for what Demosthenes
had talked himself into believing. His secondary charges are
also in some cases equally unsubstantial and flatly denied by
Aeschines. The allegation, for example, that Aeschines had mis-
treated a freeborn woman of Olynthus (196) is sheer spite;
Aeschines says in reply (4) that the audience shouted down
the charge as it was made. Among the more serious indictments
are, first, that Aeschines and the other ambassadors, this time
not including Demosthenes, deliberately tarried on the trip to
exact the oath to the treaty from Philip, although it was desira-

ble to ratify the treaty as soon as possible; second, that Aeschines promised the Athenians that Philip would respect Phocis and move against Thebes, when in fact he did just the opposite. The first charge is easier to answer: it had no doubt been perfectly clear to the ambassadors and many other Athenians that Philip simply was not going to swear until he had accomplished certain preliminaries. This is shown by the slowness with which he took the oaths when the ambassadors did meet him. The ambassadors need not have been bribed to realize that following Philip around when he was not minded to see them would not increase their influence. Aeschines says (97 f.) that a journey straight to Philip in Thrace was not part of the instructions and that the ambassadors could not have reached Philip before he left Thrace. To the second charge, that he made the assembly promises on behalf of Philip, Aeschines replies with a flat denial. It seems unlikely that a seasoned diplomat would have promised anything on behalf of a foreign king, but Aeschines on other occasions was carried away with himself and he may have said more than he intended or have been deceived by Philip. It is as possible that Demosthenes regarded Aeschines' unofficial explanation of Philip's probable intentions as a "promise" and felt that the assembly had been hoodwinked.

Another unattractive feature of the speech, and of several speeches of Demosthenes, is the personal attack on the background, private life, or appearance of an opponent. Aeschines' mother and father and his career as an actor are frequently mentioned to discredit him. Aeschines, of course, makes similar attacks on Demosthenes. These techniques reflect the fourth-century interest in personality and are a kind of perverted ethos.[17] To Demosthenes some explanation of the wickedness of Aeschines must be found, and it seems probable to associate it with his background and upbringing.

Aeschines made a very creditable reply to Demosthenes' attack and was acquitted, quite rightly. The bad blood between the two continued, however, and produced years later (330)

[17] Cf. Bruns, *op. cit.*, supra n. 18, pp. 557 ff., and T. B. L. Webster, *Art and Literature in Fourth Century Athens* (London: Athlone, 1956), pp. 85 ff. and esp. 98 ff.

the most celebrated oratorical duel of antiquity, Aeschines' *Against Ctesiphon* answered by Demosthenes' *On the Crown*. The latter of the two has traditionally been venerated as the masterpiece not only of its author but of ancient eloquence and perhaps of the spoken word. Such a judgment, of course, cannot be proved, though it may possibly be true. Twentieth-century students on first reading the speech often are not greatly moved, but then they are rarely conditioned to respond to any oratory. The critic who reads and rereads frequently ends by embracing the verdict of the centuries. In any event, *On the Crown* is a splendid compendium of all those features which in other speeches seem most characteristic of Demosthenes.

Aeschines' Speech *Against Ctesiphon*

(an abstract)

by Donovan J. Ochs

The Career of Aeschines

The sources of biographical data for Aeschines are essentially restricted to his three extant speeches *Against Timarchus*, *On the Embassy*, and *Against Ctesiphon*—and the orations of his rival, Demosthenes. From these sources we know that of the two men Aeschines was older. His birth is placed between 403 and 390 B.C. Demosthenes was born in 384 B.C.[1] When the

[1] Another primary, though less trustworthy source for the life of Aeschines is the dual biography in Plutarch's *Lives of the Ten Orators*. An account of Demosthenes' life can be read on pages 3–27 of this book. Among modern digests which treat of Aeschines' life I suggest: George Kennedy, *The Art of Persuasion in Greece* (Princeton, N.J.: Princeton University Press, 1963), pp. 236–245; *The Speeches of Aeschines*, trans. by Charles Darwin Adams (Cambridge: Harvard University Press, 1919), pp. vii–xxiii. Essentially the same material can be found in Thalheim, "Aischines," in *Paulys Realencyclopaedie der classischen Altertumwissenschaft* (Stuttgart: Alfred Druckenmueller Verlag, 1959 rep.), I.1.1050–1062; and *Discourse [par] Eschines*, Texte etabli et traduit par Victor Martin et Guy de Bude (Paris: Les Belles lettres, 1962 rep.). Cf. Friedrich Blass, *Die Attische Beredsamkeit* (Hildesheim: Georg Olms Verlagsbuchhandlung, 1962) and Arnold Schaefer, *Demosthenes und seine Zeit* (Leipzig: Teubner, 1858).

Crown speeches were given, therefore, Demosthenes was fifty-four years old, Aeschines well over sixty. The careers of both orators are curiously similar and their bitter encounters may be explained, in part, by this similarity.

Demosthenes' father, a member of the Athenian aristocracy, owned an armament industry. He died when Demosthenes was seven. The court-appointed trustees squandered the youth's inheritance, so Demosthenes' yearly education was seriously restricted by lack of funds and by poor health. In 367 B.C., we are told, after hearing the orator Callistratus successfully argue a lawsuit, Demosthenes became enamored of the power of oratory. Resolving to recover his patrimony, Demosthenes studied the art of speechmaking with Isaeus, a sophist whose specialty was testamentary law. Demosthenes won a series of five lawsuits and did regain a portion of his inheritance. His feeble voice, labored breathing, ungainly gestures, and confusing sentence structure were ridiculed when Demosthenes first spoke to the Athenian Assembly. Enlisting the aid of Satyrus, an actor, and subjecting himself to severe self-discipline,[2] he perfected his delivery, re-entered the political arena, and, as Philip's major opponent, became famous as the greatest speaker the Greek nation ever produced.

Aeschines' father returned to Athens, after suffering financial ruin in the Peloponnesian War and subsequent exile, to open a school. Aeschines taught for some years with his father, then served as a soldier in the war with Thebes. In a later campaign at Tamynae he was cited for bravery. By profession, however, Aeschines was a tragic actor of no mean ability.[3]

---

[2] The accounts of Demetrius, Phalereus, and Plutarch are possible exaggerations. Nonetheless, it is conceivable that Demosthenes may have rehearsed with pebbles in his mouth to correct his enunciation, or rehearsed before a mirror to improve his gestures, or declaimed while running up steps to increase his lung capacity, or spoken against the crashing waves to reinforce his concentration. Quite probably Demosthenes did copy and declaim the speeches in Thucydides, since numerous stylistic similarities exist. To a modern reader, however, such concern with delivery may seem overzealous, if not pathological. Parallels, however, can be found in the aberrations of the nineteenth-century elocutionists.

[3] Insufficient attention has been given to the implications of Aeschines' dramatic training. Adams remarks that, "as an actor he fell just short of the highest attainments." Thalheim refers briefly to Aeschines' "schoenen und volltoenenden Stimme." Kennedy, however, does admit that "as an

After leaving the stage he became a court clerk and, when Philip destroyed Olynthus (348 B.C.), Aeschines was elected ambassador to Arcadia.

Shortly afterward Aeschines—politically a conservative and, therefore, an advocate of peace with Philip—traveled with Demosthenes, then leader of the war faction. The purpose of their mission was to negotiate a treaty with Philip. Although the machinations and intrigue that surround the events of this first embassy, the Macedonian mission to Athens, and the ratification of the Peace of Philocrates are still disputed,[4] the following account seems most probable.

On the first proposal to Philip, Aeschines did side with Demosthenes in opposition to the terms of Philocrates' peace negotiations. A day later both orators reversed their commitments, endorsed Philocrates' proposal, and returned to Athens believing that Philip would attack Thebes, then an enemy of Athens. Both men were, of course, woefully deceived. Philip captured Phocis, an enemy of Thebes, and negotiated a treaty of unification between Thebes and Macedonia thereby creating a balance of power unfavorable to Athens.

Amid the subsequent deliberations of the Amphictyonic Council, a loosely organized group of Greek states, Aeschines successfully argued that revenge against the Phocians be mitigated. The Phocians had desecrated the temple at Delphi, and it is a tribute to Aeschines' oratorical ability that he was able to allay the indignation of the Council. At the conclusion of this meeting, Philip, one of the Council members, held a celebration attended by Aeschines and other Athenians. Aeschines was, therefore, implicated as a traitor for his attendance and indicted as such by Timarchus at the prompting of Demosthenes. Only by delaying the trial and successfully arguing a

---

actor he probably knew more about delivery than most." Fourth-century actors endured a physical regimen not unlike our best professional athletes. The demands on their voice and movement were, by our standards, incredibly severe. Cf. Peter D. Arnott, *An Introduction to the Greek Theatre* (Bloomington: Indiana University Press, 1959), Ch. III.

[4] Cf. G. L. Cawkwell, "Demosthenes' Policy After the Peace of Philocrates," *Classical Quarterly*, XIII (1963), 120–138. Also, A. W. Pickard-Cambridge, *Demosthenes and the Last Days of Greek Freedom* (New York: G. P. Putnam's Sons, 1914), Ch. VIII.

counter-indictment against the youthful profligacy of Timarchus was Aeschines able to regain partial support from the Athenians.

In 343 B.C. Demosthenes himself charged Aeschines with treason in the trial, *On the Embassy*. Neither orator won. Demosthenes lost the case, Aeschines much of his popular support. Four years later Aeschines, acting as an unofficial delegate to the Amphictyonic Council, advocated a holy war against Amphissa on the grounds that the Amphisseans were living on and cultivating cursed soil. Demosthenes opposed Aeschines' policy, realizing that such a war would provide Philip an opportunity to split central Greece. The Council voted for war. Shortly thereafter Athens and Thebes confronted Philip at Chaeronea in 338 B.C. The Macedonian won.

In 336 Aeschines indicted Ctesiphon who had proposed that Athens honor Demosthenes with a golden crown for his service to the state. Immediately after Chaeronea the Athenians had decided to rebuild and strengthen the city's walls. Demosthenes was elected by his deme [district] to oversee the repairs on their portion of the city's fortifications. Approximately ten talents from the state treasury were entrusted to Demosthenes to which sum Demosthenes added funds of his own.

While the project was underway in 336, Ctesiphon, as a gesture of friendship and admiration, proposed that Demosthenes be granted a gold crown in recognition of his services.

Martin and Bude have reconstructed Ctesiphon's proposal to read as follows:

> Since Demosthenes, in the capacity of an inspector of fortifications, has conscientiously had ditches dug along the wall and has contributed for this work a sum of 100 minae from his own means, the people resolve to award him praise and to crown him with a gold crown. The herald will proclaim at the Athenian festival of Dionysius that the people of Athens crown Demosthenes for his virtue and good will, because he continues to act and to speak for the greatest good of the people and because he has shown himself zealous in doing all the good he can.[5]

Similar proposals had been successfully made for other Athenian leaders in 340 and 338 B.C.; therefore, precedents did

[5] Martin and Bude, p. 9.

exist. Ctesiphon's bill was first presented to the Athenian Council and was approved. When the draft of the proposal reached the popular Assembly in 336, Aeschines declared it to be illegal and stated that he would indict Ctesiphon on the basis of three illegalities in the decree.

First, Aeschines charged that Ctesiphon proposed to crown Demosthenes before Demosthenes' magistracy had been audited. Athenian law did prohibit granting of honors to an accountable magistrate. Second, the location for the proclamation contradicted a law which specified that Crowns conferred by the people be proclaimed only in the Assembly. Finally, Aeschines claimed that the proposal was contrary to the truth, specifically, that Demosthenes had not always acted for the public good.

From a legal point of view Aeschines had the letter of the law on his side for the first two accusations. These laws, however, were infrequently invoked and numerous precedents authorized or at least excused Ctesiphon's proposal. Demosthenes himself had twice received a Crown at the theater as a result of decrees similar to Ctesiphon's. The third accusation, that Demosthenes had not always acted for the public good, was, in fact, the central issue. If the jury concurred with Aeschines, then part of the odium surrounding the embassy trial would be removed and Aeschines would be revenged.

Six years elapsed before the trial was held. In this period (336–330 B.C.) Philip was assassinated, Alexander took command of the Macedonian forces, and, by destroying Thebes, the young king secured a fearful respect from the Greek states.

Those who attended the Crown trial, either as jurors or mere listeners, had probably heard rumors about Alexander's defeat of Darius and the Persians. In short, Demosthenes had the difficult task of defending his unsuccessful anti-Macedonian policy when Macedonian influence encompassed most of the world.

No record remains to indicate the number of jurors who decided the Crown trial. We surmise that at least several hundred jurors' dicasts were involved. Both speakers address themselves to the "Athenians," the formula used in the popular Assembly. The two orators undoubtedly spoke as much for the crowd of listeners outside the court as for the tribunal itself. Aeschines, since he was the accuser, spoke first.

Abstract of Aeschines' Speech, *Against Ctesiphon.*

In the following abstract,[6] *the style of the first person narrative is retained to heighten the immediacy and urgency which seems to typify the speech. The abbreviations D. and Ct. are used to signify Demosthenes and Ctesiphon, respectively.*

Athenians, we can and have seen attempts made to halt this trial. I, however, rely upon the gods, the laws, and you judges. The old legal procedures would be helpful now, but the old ways have been abolished by intrigue and intimidation; therefore, restraint of public speakers is no longer possible. Nevertheless, we do retain the right to prosecute for violation of laws.

Of the forms of government democracy alone depends upon upholding established laws. If, therefore, you prosecute a violation of the law, you are upholding democracy. Be ashamed, therefore, to desert your station as defenders of democracy. If you convict *Ct.* for making an illegal proposal, you will decree what is just, what is consistent with your oaths, and advantageous to you and the entire state.

I wish to speak about the laws concerning accountable persons. A law exists forbidding anyone to crown a state official before he is audited. This law can be circumvented by appending the clause, "after he is examined by the magistrates," to their proposal. But *Ct.* transgresses the law, dispenses with the circumvention, and proposes a Crown for *D.* before the audit.

D. will argue that he was a commissioner and not a magistrate, and, therefore, not accountable. But your law reads that inspectors are to be considered magistrates, and *D.* was an inspector. Therefore, *D.* is a magistrate and falls under the law. The more ingeniously anyone may speak proposing illegal measures, so let him incur greater resentment.

D. will argue that he is guilty only of giving generously of his own funds. But in our state any public servant must make an accounting, in short, anyone who receives or spends or inter-

[6] The abstract is based on Martin and Bude's edition of the text.

feres with public affairs must be audited. Consequently, *D.* must follow the law and be audited if we wish to maintain our democracy.

Was *D.* in fact accountable? The Senate calendar shows him to be the magistrate over the theatrical funds when the Crown was proposed. *D.* was also inspector of public works at the time of the proposal. In this capacity he managed the public funds, fined other magistrates, and had the privilege of the courts; consequently, he is accountable.

D. will argue that he was neither appointed by lot nor chosen by the people. Yet the law states that any person appointed by a deme shall be considered a magistrate and the Pandionian deme appointed *D.* magistrate and inspector in addition to giving him ten talents of gold. Our law prohibits such a person from receiving a Crown without an audit.

The proclamation of the Crown is also illegal. The law clearly states that if the senate awards a Crown to anyone, the proclamation must take place in the senate. If the people award a Crown, the proclamation shall be made in the Assembly, because anyone so honored should not be pompously displayed to foreigners. *Ct.*, however, desires that the proclamation take place in the theater before the entire Greek nation.

D. will argue that contradictory laws exist on this question. But the Thesmothetae annually check the laws to eliminate contradictions. If we examine the so-called contradictory law, we find, in fact, that it refers to those persons crowned without a decree by their own demes. Such a proclamation is illegal in the theater.

Since it is also illegal, to insert falsehoods into decrees, I now turn to *D.*'s pretense for being crowned.

Consider the life of *D.* He is the man who attacked his own kinsman, Demomelas; he prosecuted his general and friend, Cephisodotus; and he is the man who lost the case to Midias for thirty minae. I will consider his life in four periods: from the war with Philip to the Peace of Philocrates; the Peace; the resumption of the war to the battle of Chaeronea; and the present.

In the first period *D.* and Philocrates flattered Philip and betrayed the king of Thrace to Philip. When Philocrates was impeached, *D.* successfully defended the culprit. On the peace mission to Philip, *D.* argued and won the provision that each Greek state should conclude a separate alliance with Philip. On his return to Athens, *D.* so hurried the Assembly into ratifying his proposal, that when the decree was approved, Thrace was absent; and therefore, Thrace was excluded from the negotiations. Then when Philip's ambassadors came to Athens, *D.* gave these enemies cushions, carpets, and front seats in the theater, and he subsequently escorted the Macedonian embassy to Thebes. Shortly afterwards *D.* pretended to see visions of Philip's death. Another example of his questionable character is that he also is guilty of offering sacrifices before performing the funeral rites for his own daughter.

During the Peace of Philocrates, as Philip moved to Phocia and Thebes, the people became angry with Philocrates and *D.*, in an attempt to be on the winning side, betrayed and turned on his fellow ministers. Then, *D.* caused our alliance with Euboea and Thebes, with the Calcidians, and with Callias. We have suffered from each of these alliances; *D.* has profited.

In the third period, prior to the battle at Chaeronea, *D.* destroyed the interests of the Greeks and of the state. He offended the gods by refusing to punish the Amphisseans who farmed the cursed land in the Cirrhaeen plain. Therefore *D.* rejects our oaths and imprecations and the oracle which decreed that anyone farming the Cirrhaeen plain shall be punished. As a result of his immorality our forces, land and sea and whole cities, have been utterly destroyed because of this man's administration.

None of our best orators could persuade Thebes to join an alliance with us. Thebes was in danger, Athens was able to ally with that nation; but it was the crisis of affairs and terror, not *D.*, that brought Athens to Thebes.

Let me consider *D.*'s offenses against you, Athenians. After pretending that the alliance with Thebes was his doing, he allowed the financial burden of the war to fall on Athens. Rather than seek peace with Philip, *D.* sent the Thebans to fight, and they were killed. Imagine his coronation ceremony in the sight of the orphans whose parents he urged to their death.

In the fourth period *D.* abandoned his post in the field and took money from the state and from the Greeks. He then attempted to insinuate himself to Alexander. If *D.* was hostilely disposed toward Alexander, he should have urged an alliance with Persia, or capitalized on Darius' military successes, or advocated engagement of the enemy when the Macedonians were cut off at Corragus. *D.* did nothing.

Consider also the life of Demosthenes. A true friend of freedom will have freeborn parents, ancestors who served the people, temperate and moderate habits, the ability to speak powerfully, and manliness of spirit. However, *D.*'s mother was the granddaughter of Gylo, a traitor, and a Scythian woman; therefore, *D.* is not actually a native Greek. *D.* squandered his paternal inheritance and now supports his life, not from his own revenues, but from dangers you risk. He is powerful in speaking, profligate in his life. Recall that Solon decreed that men who leave their posts are criminals, and recall also that cowards are legally prohibited from being crowned and taking part in public sacrifices. Therefore, when *D.* refutes my charges, consider not his words, but his actions.

You must not award Crowns excessively. Honors were rare in the days of our ancestors, today they are plentiful. Should you give Crowns to athletes who please you, few will compete. Therefore, grant honors to only a few worthy persons of true political merit. Great leaders of the past—Themistocles, Miltiades, Aristides—neither sought nor received Crowns since they did not think it necessary to be honored in the public records. *D.* will claim that my analogy is false, but one seeking honor contests against virtue, not another person.

In the past those proposing illegal measures were strictly censured, but today a defendant is concerned only with precedents of acquittal. Remember that anyone who enables a defendant to propose illegal measures destroys the constitution.

When *Ct.* comes up to speak, force him to dwell on the indictment. If you call for *D.*, you do so against the laws and the constitution. If you do call *D.*, have him use the same order I used—namely, have him discuss the laws prohibiting accountable persons from being crowned, for I have shown that *Ct.* proposed *D.*'s Crown while *D.* was still accountable. Then make *D.* discuss the illegality of the people crowning a person outside the Assembly. Then insist that *D.* discuss his private and public acts of injustice. If *D.* uses any other arrangement, he will do so only to baffle you.

If *D.* argues that such a procedure is unfair, remind him that our democracy was founded on the type of fairness that *I* ask. If he argues that he is truthful merely because he has taken an oath, remind him that an habitual perjurer requires either new gods or a new audience to gain credibility. If *D.* argues that he ought not to be banished because he has nowhere to go, ask him where Athens can go, now that he has ruined the State. Do not be moved to tears by his tears or his threats of suicide; if he were sincere, he would decline the Crown.

Ct. is not to be trusted either. You know him to go about the forum saying that he will probably be freed because of inexperience, but that he worries about the corruption of *D. D.*, however, says that he is confident of himself, but fears *Ct.*'s iniquity.

All the calumnies that *D.* will hurl at me are false. He will say that the woes of the State resulted from my speeches, but I would deliver the same speeches again. Or, he will say I was silent, but moderation caused my silence. He will say I indicted him just to please Alexander, but I did so when Philip was still alive. He will say I should have censured each act of his administration, but I speak at intervals because it is a principle of democracy to do so and such is the characteristic of men who speak only when it is expedient. He will say that like a good doctor, he prescribed what he could to save the State, but his lies and treacherous acts prevented others from speaking when the State might have been saved. And yet such a man demands honors.

On what basis should *D.* be crowned? He fortified the walls by demolishing the public tombs, he was corrupt in his dealings with regard to the Amphisseans and Euboeans, he frequently took bribes, and now his only means of defense is self-praise. If you honor *D.*, you disgrace yourselves and those who have died for our country. Public proclamations serve to instruct our youth. If you honor *D.*, you present an example of corruption to our youth. Therefore, punish *Ct.* and our youth are instructed.

When *D.* concludes his speech, imagine Solon and Aristides asking how it is that you condemned Arthmius, a man who did comparatively little wrong, and yet you consider honoring *D.*

> Be ye my witnesses, O Earth and Sun, and Virtue, and Conscience, and Education, by which we distinguish the honorable and the base, that I have heard my country's call, and have spoken. If I have presented the accusations well and in a manner commensurate with the crime, I have spoken according to my desire; if insufficiently, according to my ability. It remains for you, fellow citizens, in view both of what has been spoken and what is left unsaid, yourselves to give the verdict that is just and for the city's good.[7]

[7] Adam's translation, section 260.

Demosthenes' *Oration On the Crown*

(a translation)

by John J. Keaney

Translator's Note

This translation is based on the editions of the speech by
S. H. Butcher, Demosthenis Orationes I (*Oxford, 1903*) and,
with commentary, by W. W. Goodwin, Demosthenes, De
Corona (*Cambridge, 1901*). Where the texts differ, I have
usually preferred the readings chosen by Goodwin.

The medieval manuscripts of this and other speeches by
Demosthenes also contain documents to which Demosthenes
refers in the course of his argument—e.g., Decrees, Letters of
Philip, the Epigram of Section 289—which were read aloud in
court. It has long been recognized, however, that these documents, in the form in which they have been transmitted, are
ancient forgeries (and many of them, to use Goodwin's phrase,
ignorant forgeries) which were inserted into the text when the
original documents had been lost. They have been omitted
from the text and replaced by headings which tell what the
original documents contained and where they stood in the delivered speech.

(1)* My first words, men of Athens, are a prayer to all our gods and goddesses that in this trial I may depend on as much good will from you as I have continually maintained toward our city and toward all of you; secondly—something which concerns your piety and your reputation to the highest degree—I pray the gods to implant in your minds the thought that you should not let my opponent advise you of the manner in which you should listen to me (for that would be harsh) (2) but that you be guided by the laws and your oath, which imposes the special obligation upon you to listen to both parties in the same manner. This means not only that you should make no prejudgment, nor even that you should give both parties an equal share of your good will; it means that you should allow each party in the trial to use the type of defense he has chosen and to arrange his defense as he wishes.

(3) In this trial, Aeschines has many advantages over me, but there are two important ones, men of Athens. The first is that the result of the trial cannot have the same meaning to both of us, for it is not the same thing for me to fail to achieve your good will and for him to fail in his prosecution, while for me—I don't wish to say anything offensive at the beginning of my speech, but he accuses me from a superior position. Secondly, it is a natural characteristic of all men to enjoy listening to insults and accusations, but to be offended when they hear men praising themselves. (4) The pleasurable side is given to Aeschines, the part which irritates nearly everybody is left for me. If, to prevent this, I do not mention my achievements, I will seem to have no way of acquitting myself of the charges nor of pointing out the grounds for my claim that I deserve to be honored. But if I take up my actions and public policies, I will necessarily have to talk about myself frequently. I will attempt to do so as moderately as possible, but it is fair that Aeschines, who instituted this trial, bear the responsibility for whatever the situation itself compels me to say.

(5) I think all of you would agree that Ctesiphon and I are equally involved in this trial, and that it requires no less con-

---

* Numbers in parentheses refer to the traditional divisions of the text of the speech. Later references to the speech will use these section numbers as guides to the reader. [Editor's note.]

cern on my part. For it is a painful and cruel experience to be deprived of anything, especially if one's enemy is responsible; but it is particularly so to be deprived of your good will and affection, as to obtain these is the highest blessing. Since these are the issues in the trial, (6) I expect and ask to receive a fair hearing from all of you alike when I defend myself against the accusations, as indeed the laws require. It was Solon, a benevolent supporter of popular government, who was the original author of these laws, and he thought their validity should lie not only in the fact that they were enacted but also in that an oath was imposed on the jurors; his motive was not, it seems to me, mistrust of you, (7) but he saw that it was not possible for a defendant to avoid false and slanderous accusations—a strong advantage the prosecutor has since he addresses you first —unless each of you jurors, by preserving your piety toward the gods, would receive with good will the just arguments of the second speaker and would make your decision about the entire case on the basis of an equal and impartial hearing of both speakers.

(8) Since I am about to give an account of the whole of my personal life, it seems, today, as well as of my public policies, I wish again to invoke the gods and, in your presence, to pray, first, that in this trial I may depend on as much good will from you as I have continually maintained toward our city and toward all of you; secondly, that the gods may implant in you the ability to make a decision about this indictment which will prove to be conducive to the good reputation of all of you and the religious piety of each.

(9) If Aeschines had limited his accusations to the items contained in his indictment, I, too, would begin my defense with the Council's decree. But since he has spent at least as much of his time in discussing other matters, and mostly in lies about me, I think it at once necessary and fair that I speak briefly about these matters first, so that none of you be induced by arguments extraneous to the indictment to give an unfavorable hearing to the justice of my answer to it.

(10) See how simple and fair is my reply to the abusive slanders he has voiced at my personal life. If you know me to be the type of man he has accused me of being (for I have

never lived anywhere but among you), do not tolerate the sound of my voice, not even if my statesmanship has been brilliantly successful, but stand up and condemn me now. But if you have always assumed and have personal knowledge that I (and my family) are far better, and better born, than he and inferior to none of our respectable citizens—to avoid an invidious term—do not trust what he says about other matters (clearly it is all woven from the same fabric) but grant me today also the same good will you have shown me in many previous trials.

(11) The duplicity of your character, Aeschines, has led you to the thoroughly simple notion that I would have to reply to your abuse and neglect to discuss my public actions and policies. I shall not do it; I am not so demented. I will review my policies, the subject of your abusive falsehoods, and will take up later your loose insults—language worthy of peasant women at a comic festival—if these jurors are willing to listen to them.

(12) I have been accused of many crimes, for some of which the laws provide grave and extreme penalties. But his purpose in this trial is not that: it is to allow an enemy to heap upon me spite, malice, abuse, dirt, and everything of the kind. The city cannot come close to exacting a penalty of the sort demanded by his charges and accusations, if they were, in fact, true. (13) To prevent me from appearing before the people and obtaining a hearing from them—and this because of his spite and his envy—is, by the gods, not right or constitutional or just, men of Athens. If he saw me committing crimes against our city which were as enormous as he has just described them in his theatrical style, he had an obligation to use the penalties which the laws provide when the crimes were being committed; if he saw that my actions deserved impeachment, by impeaching me and using this procedure for settling the matter in your courts; if I was proposing illegal measures, by indicting me on these grounds. For surely it cannot be that he is prosecuting Ctesiphon through me, but that he would not have indicted me, if he thought he could convict me. (14) Furthermore, if he saw me doing any of the other things with which he has now slandered me or any crime whatsoever against you, there are laws and punishments for all of them; there are proc-

esses and suits which carry grave and severe penalties, and all
of these he could have used; if he had ever clearly done this
and had taken advantage of such possible measures against me,
his accusation now would be consistent with his behavior in the
past. (15) As it is, he has stepped off the path of right and
justice and avoided investigating my actions at the time they
were done; he is playing a stage part, piling up charges and
jokes and abuse much after the events. In the second place, he
accuses me, but brings Ctesiphon to trial; his enmity toward
me is the pre-eminent feature of this whole trial but, never dar-
ing to meet me on that ground, he clearly seeks to deprive another man of his civic rights. (16) Yet, men of Athens, besides
all the other arguments one could cite in support of Ctesiphon,
it seems to me that one could say with much justice that it was
fair for Aeschines and me to settle our personal feuds by ourselves, not to dismiss a personal confrontation and look for a
third party to cause trouble to. This is the height of injustice.

(17) All of his accusations alike, one may see, are neither
just nor based on the truth. I wish to examine them one by one,
and especially the lies he has told about me in the matter of the
Peace and the embassy, attributing to me what he himself did
in conjunction with Philocrates. It is necessary, men of Athens,
and fitting as well that I remind you of the chronology of the
events so that you may observe each event in its temporal context.

(18) When the Phocian War broke out (I was not to
blame for this; at that time I had not entered public life),
your first reaction was to desire the safety of the Phocians, although you saw that some of their actions were unjust, and to
enjoy whatever trouble came to the Thebans—your anger
against them was neither unreasonable nor unfair, since they
had made immoderate use of their successes at Leuktra. Further, the whole of the Peloponnese was in dissension, the most
bitter enemies of the Spartans were not strong enough to destroy them, those who formerly ruled through the influence of
the Spartans were not in control of their cities, but there was a
kind of strife-ridden confusion among these peoples and among
the rest of the Greeks which did not admit of settlement. (19)
When Philip saw the situation (it wasn't hard to see), he em-

broiled and stirred them up against each other by lavishing bribes on the traitors in each city. He prepared himself to take advantage of others' blunders and errors of judgment and was becoming a threat to all. Exhausted by the length of the war, the Thebans—once overbearing, now luckless—were clearly being forced to have recourse to you; Philip, to prevent this and to prevent our cities joining together, offered peace to you and assistance to them. (20) What ally did he have to trap you almost into deceiving yourselves? It was—shall I call it the cowardice or the ignorance or both of the rest of the Greeks, who did not provide men or money or anything to help you although you were fighting a long and drawn-out war, and this for the benefit of all of them, as later experience made clear. Your anger at them was just and deserved, and you were ready to listen to Philip. And so we acquiesced in the Peace for these reasons—not because of me, as Aeschines has falsely charged— and it was made. If one examines fairly the crimes and venalities of these men in the matter of the Peace, he will find that they are responsible for the present state of affairs. (21) It is for the sake of the truth that I go through all these facts in detail. For if it should become evident that there was wrong-doing, it has, of course, nothing to do with me. The first to mention and suggest the Peace was Aristodemos, the tragic actor; Philocrates of Hagnous, who took up the cue, proposed the peace and hired himself for this purpose—your associate, Aeschines, not mine—not even if you burst a blood vessel lying about it; the ones who joined this proposal (for whatever motives, I omit this for the present) were Euboulos and Kephisophon. I had nothing to do with any of it.

(22) Although these are facts and are supported by the truth, Aeschines reached the limit of shamelessness when he dared to say that, in addition to being responsible for the Peace, I also prevented the city from making the Peace in consultation with the rest of Greece. Then, you—what is the proper word to describe you? When was it that you, with your own eyes, saw me depriving Athens of so important an enterprise, so beneficial an alliance as you have described it, when was it that you became indignant or came forward and revealed in detail what you are now accusing me of? (23) If I

had sold out to Philip the means to prevent Greece uniting, it was your duty not to be silent, but to cry aloud, to protest, to reveal it to these citizens. You never did this, no one heard you say this. No embassy was visiting any Greek state at the time, but all states had been canvassed long before, and nothing Aeschines has said on the matter is sound. (24) Apart from this, it is the city which is the chief victim of his false slanders. For if you were summoning the Greeks to war, while at the same time you were sending ambassadors to discuss peace with Philip, that was an act worthy of Eurybatos, not of a city, nor of honorable men. It simply is not so. What purpose could you have had in sending ambassadors at that stage of the crisis? Peace? It was available to everybody. War? The topic of your own deliberations was peace. Clearly I was not the author of the Peace in the beginning, nor responsible for it, nor is any of his other accusations against me shown to be true.

(25) When the city agreed to the Peace, consider again the policies each of us chose. From these you will learn who was Philip's ally in all areas of the struggle, and who acted in your behalf and sought the advantage of Athens. As a member of the Council, I introduced a motion that the ambassadors should find out where Philip was and sail there as quickly as possible to administer the oath. They were unwilling to do this, even when I had the motion approved. (26) What did this mean, men of Athens? I will tell you. It was to Philip's advantage that the longest possible time should intervene before the oath was administered, but to your interest that the time be the shortest possible. Why? Because you broke off all your preparations for war not only from the day on which you swore the oath but from the day on which you expected that there would be peace; for all this time, he was busy preparing for war, believing—as was true—that whatever possessions of the city he could acquire before the oath was administered would be firmly in his control. No one, he thought, would abrogate the Peace for the sake of these places. (27) I foresaw this result, men of Athens, and this was the reasoning behind my motion of the decree that they should sail to wherever Philip was and administer the oath as quickly as possible, so that the oath would take effect while the Thracians, your allies, still held the

places which Aeschines was ridiculing just now, Serrion and Myrtenon and Ergiske; so that Philip would not establish control of Thrace by seizing strategic areas; and so that he would not, with the large supply of money and soldiery so gained, interfere in our future affairs. (28) Aeschines does not discuss this motion nor does he have it read to you; rather he attempts to defame me with the charge that, as a member of the Council, I thought that the ambassadors should be introduced to your Assembly. How should I have acted? Should I not have motioned that they be brought to negotiate the peace with you, when this was their purpose in coming? Or, should I not have instructed the manager to give them seats at the dramatic festival? But they would have watched from the inexpensive seats, if this motion was not made. Should I have guarded the minor interests of the State and sold out, as these did, its main interest? Of course not. Read, please, this decree, which Aeschines has passed over, although he clearly knows of its existence.

DECREE (29)

(30) Although I proposed this decree then and sought the city's benefit, not Philip's, our noble ambassadors, who couldn't have cared less, sat in Macedonia for three whole months until Philip returned after subjugating all of Thrace; it was possible for them to have arrived at the Hellespont and save those places within ten days, perhaps within three or four, by administering the oaths before they were seized by Philip. For, if our representatives were there, he would not have laid a hand on the places; else, we would not have administered the oath, with the result that he would have failed to gain the Peace, and would not now have both, the Peace and the territory.

(31) It was in the embassy, then, that Philip played his first trick and these unjust men took their first bribe. In this matter, I avow that I am opposed to them and at war with them, then and now and in the future. But look at another act, still more criminal than this, which took place right afterwards. (32) When Philip swore to the Peace, after he had already taken Thrace through the reluctance of the ambassadors to obey my proposal, he bribed them again, not to leave Macedo-

nia until he had completed preparations for an expedition against the Phocians; his purpose was that, while we were reporting here his intention and preparations to march, you would not sail to Pylae with warships and close off the area, as you had done before, but that, at the same time you were listening to our report, you would hear that he was inside Pylae and there was nothing you could do. (33) Although he had already seized the places he had, so fearful and anxious was Philip that control of events might escape him if you should decide to send aid before Phocis was lost, that he hired this contemptible Aeschines, not now in union with the rest of the ambassadors but singly, by himself, to make the kind of reports to you which caused the loss of everything. (34) I think you should—I beg you—remember throughout this trial, men of Athens, that if Aeschines had not charged me with matters not contained in the indictment, I would not be answering in kind. But, since he has made all sorts of defamatory charges, I also must make a brief reply to each of his accusations. (35) What did he say in the speeches delivered by him at the time, speeches through which everything was lost? "That there is no need to be disturbed by Philip's arrival at Pylae; everything will work out to your desire; you will hear in two or three days that Philip has proved to be a friend of those to whom he came as an enemy, and an enemy of those to whom he came as a friend. It is not words," he said, "which cement relationships— how exalted his language!—but mutual interest; it is in Philip's interest and in the Phocians' and in yours, all alike to free yourselves of the oppressive brutality of the Thebans." (36) These words had a pleasant sound to some, because of the hatred of the Thebans which then existed. What happened shortly, almost immediately, after this? The Phocians were destroyed and their cities razed; you kept quiet and believed him; a little later, you moved your possessions in from the country-districts; Aeschines got his money; finally, the city received the hatred of the Thebans and Thessalians; Philip received the gratitude for the outcome of the events. (37) To prove that these are the facts, read, please, the decree of Kallisthenes and the letter of Philip; from both, all I have stated will be clear.

DECREE (38)

Were these the expectations with which you made the peace? Were these the promises which this hireling made to you?

(39) Read the letter which Philip sent afterwards.

LETTER

(40) You hear how clearly and precisely he defines matters to his allies in the letter he wrote to you. "My action was against the wishes and to the distress of the Athenians; consequently, if you are prudent, Thebans and Thessalians, you will take the Athenians to be your enemies and put your trust in me." He does not write this in so many words, but this is what he wants to make clear. Afterward, he transported them to such a peak of insensibility about any future results of his actions that they even allowed him to control all their affairs. The result is that his wretched allies enjoy their present miserable condition. (41) His assistant in this persuasion and his comrade, the one who made those false reports here and tricked you, it is he who now bewails the sufferings of the Thebans and has given us such a pitiful catalogue of them and of what the Phocians suffered and of all the other troubles of the Greeks; yet he himself is responsible for all of them. Of course you feel sorrow at what has happened, Aeschines, and pity the Thebans; you have an estate in Boeotia and farm Boeotians' land; of course I rejoice, whose person was demanded immediately by the destroyer of Thebes.

(42) But I have slipped into matters which it is, perhaps, more fitting to mention a little later. I return to my exposition of how the crimes of these men have proved to be responsible for the present state of affairs.

When you were deceived by Philip, because of his agents who had sold themselves in the embassies and reported nothing true to you, and the miserable Phocians were deceived and their towns destroyed, what ensued? (43) The contemptible Thessalians and the brutal Thebans thought Philip their friend, their benefactor, their saviour; he was everything to them, nor did they hear the voice of anyone who would say otherwise.

Suspicious and offended by what had happened, you kept the Peace nevertheless; you had no other choice. The rest of the Greeks, like you, deceived and cheated of their hopes, kept the Peace, although they had, in a certain sense, been warred against for a long time. (44) For when Philip was in the territory of the Illyrians and Triballoi, he subjugated some of the Greeks also and put under his control many large forces. Even some from our cities went there with the freedom of travel gained by the Peace and were corrupted; Aeschines was one of them. At that time, all against whom Philip was directing these preparations were in fact at war. If they were unaware of it, that is another matter and has nothing to do with me. (45) For I made solemn and public forewarnings to you, on every occasion, and wherever I was sent as ambassador. But the cities were diseased; their political leaders were corrupting themselves by taking bribes, their citizens—the majority—partly had no foresight, partly were ensnared by the indolent leisure of daily life. All alike were the victims of a similar delusion, each thinking that disaster would strike everywhere except upon himself, and that they could safeguard, whenever they wished, their own possessions because the danger would be to others. (46) Then, I think, it turned out that the citizens lost their freedom in return for their great and untimely indolence, and their leaders, who thought that they had sold out everything except themselves, found that they had sold themselves first. Instead of "friend" and "guest," the names they had when they were taking bribes, they now hear themselves called "flunkies" and "hated of the gods" and every other name which fits them. (47) For no one, men of Athens, seeks to benefit the traitor when he spends money, nor, when he has got control of what he has bought, does he use the traitor to advise him in the rest of his affairs. If it were not so, no one would lead a more blessed life than the traitor. But it is not so. How could it be? When one who desires to rule establishes control over the situation and is master of those who sold out, it is then that he recognizes their baseness, then that he hates and mistrusts and insults them. (48) Look at it in this way. Even if the opportunity to affect events has passed, the prudent always have open to them the opportunity to understand them. Lasthenes was called "friend" up to the time he betrayed Olynthus; Timolaos, up to the time he destroyed Thebes; Eudikos and Simos of Larisa, up to the time they put Thessaly in Philip's control. Then the whole world came to be filled with men like these, exiled and rootless, insulted and exposed to every calamity. What about Aristratos in Sicyon and Perillos in Megara? Were they not thrown out? (49) From such examples it is clear to see that the statesman who best guards his homeland and offers the most opposition to men like these is the one, Aeschines, who provides the opportunity to traitors and hirelings to take their bribes; it is through the majority of the citizens here and those who resisted your plans that you are safe and can earn your wages, since you would long ago have ruined yourselves, if left to your own efforts.

(50) Although I still have much to say about the events surrounding the Peace, I think what I have said is more than enough. This man is to blame, who has spewed at me the garbage of his own villainy. I must defend myself to those of you who are too young to have witnessed the events; others of you were, perhaps, irritated at my remarks, I mean those of you who knew that he had been bribed, before I said anything about it. (51) And yet he calls this bribery an act of "friendship" and just now, somewhere in his speech, referred to him "who reproaches me with the friendship of Alexander." I reproach you with the friendship of Alexander? Where did you get it from? How did you deserve it? I would not call you—I am not insane—the guest of Philip or the friend of Alexander, unless one should also call farm hands or any other kind of hireling guests and friends of their employers. (52) Before, I called you the hireling of Philip and now, the hireling of Alexander, as do all of these here. If you don't believe me, ask them, or, rather, I will do it for you. Does Aeschines seem to you, men of Athens, to be the hireling or the friend of Alexander? You hear what they say.

(53) Finally, I wish to make my defense against the indictment itself, and to discuss my activities in detail so that Aeschines, although he already knows them, will hear my reasons for saying that I have a just claim on the rewards mentioned in the

Council's resolution and much greater rewards than these. Please read the indictment.

(56) These are the details of Ctesiphon's decree, men of Athens, on which he bases his prosecution. In the first place, I think I will make clear to you, from these very details, that my whole defense will be fair. For I will use the same order of the items in the indictment as he; I will speak to each of these in order; and I will omit nothing willingly. (57) The words of Ctesiphon's proposal are that I "spoke and acted continually for the best interests of the people and was eager to do whatever good I was capable of and that I be praised for this." I believe that your judgment on the proposal should be based on my political actions. When these are examined, it will be found whether the items of Ctesiphon's proposal which concern me are true and deserved or whether they are in fact false. (58) As to the fact that Ctesiphon did not add the clause "when I pass the audit," and bade the Crown to be proclaimed in the theatre, I think that this too is connected with my political actions, that is, whether I deserve the Crown and the public proclamation or not. Further, I think that I should specify the legal basis of Ctesiphon's proposal. This is the simple and fair defense I have decided to make, and I will now proceed to my actions. (59) But let no one think that my remarks are irrelevant to the indictment, if I happen to discuss foreign policy. For the prosecutor, who has called untrue that part of the proposal which states that my actions and speeches were for the best, is the same man who has made a discussion of all my policies relevant and necessary to the charge. Secondly, of the many areas of government which were open to me, I chose the one which deals with foreign policy, so that I can fairly begin my exposition in this sphere.

(60) I will pass over what Philip seized and held before I began to make speeches on public policy. None of this, I think, has anything to do with me. I will mention and give a full account of what he was prevented from doing, beginning with the day on which I involved myself in this sphere, premising

only this much. Philip had one large advantage, men of Athens.
(61) For among the Greeks, not some but all alike, there grew
a crop of traitors and hirelings and men hateful to the gods, the
like of which no one can ever recall before. With these as his
assistants and accomplices, he worsened the relations between
the Greeks, which even before this were bad and faction-
ridden. Some he deceived, others he bribed, others he thoroughly corrupted; he split the Greeks into many factions, although they all had a single interest, to prevent him from
becoming powerful. (62) When all the Greeks were in this
state and ignorant of the growing and gathering danger, you,
men of Athens, should consider what was the proper course of
action for our city to have chosen and expect an account of this
from me. For I took my position in this area of government.
(63) Should Athens, Aeschines, denying her pride and her dignity, have taken a position with the Thessalians and Dolopi-
ans, by this act obtaining the rule of Greece for Philip and
nullifying the just and glorious deeds of our forefathers? That
was not the proper course—it is truly unthinkable—but was it
proper for Athens to allow acts to go on, which she knew long
before would take place, if no one prevented them? (64) I
would now like to ask the severest critic of our actions, on
which side he would have wanted Athens to be: on that which
shares the responsibility for the shameful and ugly results
which befell Greece (here were the Thessalians and their followers) or on the side which overlooked what was going on in
the hope of personal aggrandizement (here we would put the
Arcadians, Messenians, and Argives)? (65) But even many of
these, rather all of them, fared worse than we. If Philip, after
gaining control, had departed, kept peace afterward and
harmed none of his own allies or the rest of the Greeks, there
might be some grounds for accusing and blaming those who
opposed his actions. But if he has taken away, from all alike,
reputation, leadership, and freedom—and even the free governments of as many as he could—how could the decision you
took at my urging fail to be most glorious?

(66) I return to my question. What was the right course for
Athens, Aeschines, when it saw Philip attempting to gain for
himself tyrannical rule over Greece? What was the only policy

for a statesman at Athens—for this makes all the difference—to advise or propose, a statesman who knew that our country, throughout its history up to the day he himself ascended the speaker's platform, always fought for the first rank in honor and reputation, and had spent more men and money for the honor and benefit of all than the rest of the Greeks had spent in their own behalf, (67) a statesman who saw that Philip, with whom was our struggle, had had his eye knocked out, his collarbone broken, his hand and his leg maimed for the sake of preserving his rule, and was ready to sacrifice any part of his body which fortune would take, so that he could live the rest of his life in honor and glory? (68) Indeed no one, I suppose, would have the nerve to say that a person born in Pella, a small and graceless place in those days at least, could fittingly have born in him such greatness of spirit as to let a desire to rule Greece come into his mind, while it was proper for you, who are Athenians, who have before you every day of your lives, in everything you see and hear, memorials of the courage of your forefathers, to have such cowardice as to become eager volunteers in yielding your freedom to Philip. Not a single person would say this. (69) Therefore the only choice, and the necessary choice, left to you was justly to oppose all his unjust actions against you. This course you took from the beginning, naturally and fittingly, this course I proposed and advised in the time of my political activity. I admit it. What should I have done? Now I ask you, Aeschines, omitting everything else, Amphipolis, Pydna, Potidæa, Halonnesos. I mention none of these. (70) Serrion, Doriskos, the sacking of Peparethos, the other injustices of which our city was victim—I don't even know if they happened. Yet it was you who said that I brought Athens into the quarrel by talking about these places, although the decrees were proposed by Euboulos and Aristophon and Diopeithes, not by me—how easily you say whatever you please! But I will not talk of this now. (71) Philip, who appropriated Eubœa, who prepared to make it a fortress against Attica, who attempted to get control of Megara, who seized Oreos, who razed Porthmos, who set up the tyrants Philistides in Oreos and Kleitarchos in Eretria, who subjugated the Hellespont, who besieged Byzantium, who destroyed some Greek cities and restored exiles to others; in these actions was Philip doing wrong, and breaking treaties, and disrupting the Peace or not? Was there a need for someone to rise among the Greeks and put a stop to these actions or not? (72) If not, if Greece was to present the spectacle of Mysian booty—a prey to everyone—while there were still Athenians alive, I have wasted my efforts in talking; the city, in following my advice, has wasted its efforts; let all the actions we took be my crimes, my blunders. But if there was a need for someone to rise and put a stop to Philip, who more fittingly than the Athenian people? This was my policy: I opposed Philip when I saw him enslaving all mankind; continually I spoke out and my clear advice was, "Do not surrender!" Finally, it was Philip, not the city, Aeschines, who broke the Peace by seizing the merchant ships.

(73) Bring the decrees and the letter of Philip and read them in order. It will become clear from these documents who is responsible for what.

DECREE (74)

(75) Euboulos proposed this decree, not I, Aristophon the one after this, then Hegesippos, then Aristophon again, then Philokrates, then Kephisophon, then all together. I had nothing to do with them. Read the decrees.

DECREES

(76) As I point to these decrees, Aeschines, so you point to what decree of mine makes me responsible for the war. You won't be able to. If you could, there is nothing else you would have produced first. Even Philip does not impute any blame for the war to me, although he censures others. Read the letter of Philip.

LETTER (77–78)

(79) Nowhere in this letter does he indict Demosthenes, or attach any blame to me. When he censures others, why does he not mention my actions? Because he would have to mention his own crimes, which I watched closely and opposed. First, I proposed an embassy to the Peloponnese, as soon as he slipped into the Peloponnese, then an embassy to Euboea, when he laid

his hands on Eubœa, then a military expedition—no longer an embassy—to Oreos and one to Eretria, when he set up tyrants in those cities. (80) Afterwards, I was responsible for sending out all the naval expeditions which saved the Chersonese, Byzantium, and the rest of our allies. As a result of these actions, you received the noblest rewards from those who received your help: praise, glory, honors, crowns, gratitude. Some of the victims of his injustice—those who were persuaded by you—were rescued; the rest, who consistently depreciated your warnings, now remember them and believe not only that you had their interests at heart but were also prudent men and even prophets. For everything turned out as you predicted. (81) Everyone knows that Philistides would have spent a great deal of money to keep Oreos, Kleitarchos a great deal to keep Eretria, and Philip himself a great deal to have these two places to depend upon against Athens, to avoid exposure of the rest of his intrigues, and to prevent any general investigation of his unjust actions; everyone knows this, you most of all. (82) For when the ambassadors from Kleitarchos and Philistides came here then, they stayed with you, Aeschines, and you were their official host. They were your friends, whom the city rejected as enemies and as making proposals which were neither just nor beneficial. Nothing of the kind was successful with me, although you defame me and say that I am silent, when I have taken a bribe, and start screaming, when I have spent it. But not you. You scream all the time, and never will stop unless these jurors stop you by voting against you today. (83) On that occasion, you Athenians voted me a Crown for this policy; Aristonikos, who proposed this Crown, used the very same words in his proposal that Ctesiphon has now used; the Crown was proclaimed in the theatre—that was the second proclamation for me; Aeschines was in the assembly, but he did not speak against the proposal nor indict the proposer. Read, please, this decree too.

DECREE (84)

(85) Is there any one of you who knows of any shame or mockery or ridicule the city suffered because of this decree? These are the results he now predicts, if I am voted a Crown.

Yet, it is when the situation is fresh in everybody's mind that the adviser is rewarded with gratitude, if things go well, and is punished, if not. At the time, I clearly was rewarded with gratitude, not with censure or punishment.

(86) Up to the time these events took place, it is agreed that everything I did was for the best interests of the city, by the fact that my advice and proposals were carried when you were deliberating, by the fact that I accomplished what I proposed and thereby brought crowns to the city, to me, and to all of you, by the fact that you had sacrifices and processions to the gods because my proposals were successful.

(87) When Philip was driven out of Eubœa by you—I mean, by your weapons but as a result of my policy and decrees proposed (even if some burst a blood vessel at this) by me—he began to look for another place to be used as a fortress against Athens. He saw that we import more grain than any other people and, intending to control the grain route, he sailed to the Byzantines in Thrace, who were his allies; first, he demanded that they join him in the war against you and, when they were reluctant to do this, saying that their alliance with him was not on these terms—as was true—he built a palisade around the city, brought up artillery, and began to besiege it. (88) I will not ask what was your proper course of action when this happened. It was quite clear. But who was it who went to the aid of the Byzantines and saved them? Who was it who prevented the Hellespont from falling into his power at that time? You, men of Athens. And when I say you, I mean our city. But who was the one who spoke and proposed and, in a word, devoted himself completely to the situation? It was I. (89) You have experienced in fact, and don't need any words of mine, how much this policy benefitted everybody. Not to consider the glorious reputation it brought you, the war which then broke upon us supplied you with all the necessities of life in greater abundance and cheaper than they are in the present peace, a peace which these noble gentlemen preserve to the detriment of their country and in the hope of future personal gain; may they be cheated of that hope; may they share with you, who want what is best, the blessings which you seek from the gods; may they not have you share in the certain results of

their policies. Read for the jury the decrees of the Byzantines and Perinthians, in which they voted you Crowns.

DECREE OF THE BYZANTINES (90–91)

(92) Read also the similar decrees from the inhabitants of the Chersonese.

DECREE OF THE PEOPLE OF THE CHERSONESE

(93) The effect of my policies not only was to save the Chersonese and Byzantium, to prevent Philip from controlling the Hellespont then, and to gain distinction for our city, but it also showed to all mankind the nobility of our city and the evil of Philip. Everyone saw the ally of the people of Byzantium besieging it; what could be more shameful or more disgusting than this? (94) Although you had many just grounds of complaint for their inconsiderate conduct toward you in former times, you showed that you did not bear grudges nor abandon the victims of injustice but even saved them. As a result, you gained fame and good will from all. You know, all of you, that you have crowned many of your political leaders before now, but no one can show that it was through the efforts of anyone else—I mean as speaker and adviser—that our city was crowned, except through mine.

(95) I want to show you that the slanderous remarks he directed against the people of Eubœa and Byzantium, carefully reminding you of every unpleasant act of theirs toward you in the past, were intended to be provocative, not only because they were false (I presume you know this) but because, even if they were true, the way I handled matters was beneficial to you. I will do this by discussing one or two of the glorious actions of our city in your time, but my discussion will be brief. A man, by himself, and citizens, in common, should always attempt to base their future actions on the noblest standards of their past. (96) When the Spartans ruled on land and sea, and their governors and garrisons controlled all the areas surrounding Attica, Eubœa, Tanagra, all of Bœotia, Megara, Aegina, Keos, the other islands, when our city then had no walls, no ships, you, men of Athens, marched to Haliartos and a few days afterwards to Corinth, although the Athenians of that

time had many bad memories of what the Corinthians and Bœotians had done to them in the Decelean war. But they did not let these memories influence them, far from it. (97) Both of these marches, Aeschines, were not made to reward benefactors nor, as the Athenians saw, were they without danger. In spite of this, they did not sacrifice those who took refuge with them but they were willing to face possible catastrophe in order to preserve their honor and reputation, a correct and noble decision. Death is the end of every man's life, even if, to protect himself, a man shuts himself up in a little room. Good men must always involve themselves in every noble course, holding good hope before them as a shield, and bear in a noble spirit whatever the god sends. (98) Your forefathers did this; your elders did this when they prevented the Thebans, the victors at Leuktra, from destroying Sparta, although the Spartans were not their friends and benefactors and indeed had done many grievous wrongs to our city; they did not fear the strength of the Thebans nor the military reputation they had then, nor did they take into account what wrongs they had suffered from the people for whom they would be risking themselves. (99) With these acts, you showed all of Greece that, if someone did you harm, you would preserve your anger, but for other times; if danger to their freedom or security should come upon that people, you showed that you would not bear grudges or allow a grudge to influence you. You displayed this quality not at that time alone, but again, when the Thebans were attempting to appropriate Eubœa, you did not fail to respond: nor did you need reminding of the wrong done to you by Themison and Theodoros in the matter of Oropos, but you came even to their aid; this was the time the city first had volunteer trierarchs, and I was one of them (I will talk about this later). (100) Your action even in saving the island was noble, but still more noble was your action when, with the fate of their persons and their cities in your hands, you justly restored these to people who had wronged you, and you were not influenced by the injustice you suffered at a time when they trusted you. I pass over the innumerable other actions I could mention, the naval battles, the land expeditions—those of long ago and those of our own times—all of which our city engaged in for the freedom and security of the rest of Greece. (101) When I observed that our city voluntarily fought for the benefit of others in so many situations of this nature, what was I to bid or to advise her to do when she was deliberating about what was, in a certain sense, her own benefit? To remember past grievances, by God, against those who wanted to be rescued and to search for excuses to sacrifice everything. Who would not have killed me with justice, if I had attempted, even with words, to bring shame upon any of the noble traditions of our city? I know well that you would not have done any shameful action. If you wanted to, what stood in your way? Was it not possible? Didn't you have men like these advising such a course?

(102) Well, I wish to return to my policies after this. And think over what was best for Athens then. I saw that your fleet, men of Athens, was being broken up; that your wealthy citizens were failing their obligations by making small contributions and that those of your citizens who possessed a moderate or small amount of property were losing what they had; further, that our city was missing opportunities because of the financial situation. I submitted a law which compelled some citizens, the wealthy, to meet their obligations, stopped the oppression of the poor and—what was most useful to the city—made us prepared to meet any opportunity. (103) When the legality of this law was attacked, I came before you in that trial and was acquitted; the prosecutor did not receive a fifth of the votes. And yet, how much money do you think I was offered by those in the highest tax brackets not to submit this law for passage; or, if not that, at least to let it be suspended while its legality was being appealed? Men of Athens, I would hesitate to tell you how much it was. (104) But their attempt was reasonable. According to the former law, they could make their contribution in groups of sixteen, each contributing little or nothing, and crushing the poor citizens; according to my law, each had to pay a quota assessed on his property, and the man who formerly contributed one-sixteenth to the expense of a single trireme* now became trierarch of two. They had not even

* A trireme is a ship or galley with three banks of oars. In Athens a citizen providing the funds for outfitting a trireme was known as a trierarch. [Editor's note.]

called themselves trierarchs any longer, but joint-contributors. There is nothing they would not have offered so that this law would be abrogated and they would not be compelled to meet their just obligations.

(105) Please read the decree for which I was indicted, then the list of contributors, the one from the former law and the one according to mine.

DECREE

(106) Bring up also that noble list.

LIST

Put up beside this the list according to my law.

LIST

(107) Do you think that this was a small help to the poor, or that the rich were willing to spend only a small amount to avoid meeting their obligations? I pride myself not only that this practice was stopped and that I was acquitted when indicted but also that the law I had passed was beneficial and was proved so in fact. Throughout the war, when naval expeditions were sent out according to the provisions of my law, no trierarch ever made an appeal to law with the claim that he was being treated unjustly by you, no trierarch became a suppliant in Mounichia, no trierarch was imprisoned by the Naval Boards, no trireme was abandoned at sea and lost to the city, no trireme was left in the harbor because it was unfit to sail. (108) Yet all of these things used to happen under the former laws. The reason is that the trierarchic obligation was imposed on the poor: many of these obligations became impossible. I transferred the trierarchies from the poor to the rich. Everything now happened as it was supposed to. Moreover, I deserve praise for this, and I chose the policies which brought praise and honor and power to the city. No policy of mine was ever malicious, vindictive or malign, nor paltry, nor unworthy of Athens. (109) It will be clear that I preserved the same quality in internal policy as well as in foreign policy: in internal policy, I did not prefer favors from the rich to justice toward the poor; in for-

eign policy, I did not desire the gifts and the friendship of Philip instead of the common benefit of all Greece.

(110) It remains, I think, for me to speak about the proclamation and about the audit, for I believe that it has become sufficiently clear from what I have said that I acted for the best and that I continued to be well-minded toward you and eager to benefit you. Yet I pass over the most successful of my policies and actions, on the assumption, first, that I must speak on each of the items in the charge of illegality; secondly, that, even if I say nothing of the rest of my policies, all of you are certainly familiar with them.

(111) I think that you did not understand nor was I myself able to grasp most of the legal arguments Aeschines used; he made them thoroughly confusing by putting up details of different laws side-by-side. I will speak about the rights of the case simply and straightforwardly. I am so far from saying that I am not accountable—the gist of his slander—that I admit I am accountable throughout my life for the public monies I have handled or for my public acts. (112) As far as what I offered and gave to the people from my private resources, I claim that I am not accountable for a single day of my life (do you hear, Aeschines?), nor is anyone else, not even if he be one of the nine archons [magistrates]. What law is so thoroughly inhuman and unjust as to cause an official who gave some of his personal property and performed a humane and generous act to be robbed of gratitude, to be exposed to malicious accusers, and to put these in control of the accounts he submitted? There is no such law. If he says there is, let him point to it. I will be satisfied and will keep silent. (113) There is no such law, men of Athens; his accusation is malicious in that, because I made personal gifts of money when I was Commissioner of the Theoric Fund, he says, "Ctesiphon praised him while he was still accountable." You mention, malicious person that you are, none of the things for which I was accountable, but only my gifts. "But you were also a member of the Commission on the City Walls." For this I was rightly praised, because the expenditures were my gift and I did not claim reimbursement. A claim for reimbursement requires audits and officials to examine it, but a

free gift deserves gratitude and praise. This is why Ctesiphon made his proposal about me. (114) I will easily show with many examples that this procedure is defined in your customs as well as in your laws. In the first place, when Nausikles was a general, he was frequently crowned by you for expenditures he made from his own resources. Secondly, when Diotimos and again Charidemos contributed shields, they were crowned. Thirdly, Neoptolemos here, who was in charge of many public works, was honored for his contributions. It would be a cruel thing if a man, in any office, were not allowed to contribute to the city from his personal resources throughout his term of office or if he were subject to investigation for what he had given instead of receiving gratitude. (115) To prove that I speak the truth, please read the decrees in honor of these men.

DECREES (116)

(117) Each of these men, Aeschines, was accountable for the office he held; he was not accountable for the gifts which brought him a crown. Surely, then, I am not either. For I make the same claim as these others in the same situation. I made contributions; I am praised for these; I am not accountable for my contributions. I held office; I submitted accounts of my office, not of my contributions.

"By God (you say) you were corrupt when in office."

Why didn't you accuse me, when the examiners submitted my accounts to the court? You were there.

(118) Read the whole proposal made in my honor, that you may see that Aeschines himself bears witness to the fact that I was not crowned for acts for which I was accountable. He will prove himself a malicious accuser, because he fails to include in his charges some details of the Council's decree.

DECREE

(119) These were my personal contributions; you have indicted none of them. You admit that it is legal for the city to receive gifts, but you charge that it is illegal to express gratitude for them. What kind of man, in the eyes of the gods, would be all-wicked, hated of the gods, and utterly vindictive? Would it not be a man like this?

(120) The next item is the proclamation of the Crown in the theatre. I pass over the innumerable times innumerable Crowns were so proclaimed, and that I myself was frequently crowned in this way before. But, for heaven's sake, Aeschines, are you so imperceptive and so stupid that you cannot grasp the fact that the gift of a Crown causes the same pride in its recipient wherever it is proclaimed? And that the proclamation in the theatre assists the purposes of the donors? All who hear the proclamation are encouraged to serve their city and they praise those who confer the favor more than its recipient. This is why the city has this law. Please read the law.

LAW

(121) You hear, Aeschines, the clear statement of the law: "Except in cases which the people and Council approve: let the herald proclaim these." Why then, miserable man, do you make malicious accusations? Why do you fabricate arguments? Why don't you take hellebore to cure your madness? Do you feel no shame at bringing in a suit based on envy, not on any offense, at remaking laws and omitting parts of laws when it is only right that the whole law be read to jurors who have sworn to make their decision according to the laws? (122) You act like this, and then you list the qualities a public servant should have, just like one who contracts to have a statue made and then gets it back with the contract unfulfilled, or as if public servants were known by their words and not by their actions and policies. You scream every kind of filthy name at me, like a comic reveler from a wagon, names which suit you and your family, not me. There is also this to think of, men of Athens. (123) I believe that the difference between insult and accusation lies in this, that accusation is directed at crimes for which there are penalties in the laws, while insult involves slander, which naturally involves only the statements which personal enemies make about each other. It is my conviction that your forefathers built these courts, not so that we could collect you here to listen to men making libelous statements about each other for their own reasons, but so that we could convict anyone who has committed a crime against the city. (124) Aeschines knows this as well as I, but he has chosen to revel in slander rather than

make accusations. It is not right that he should leave without getting as much as he has given. I will now take up this point, asking him this small question. Should one say, Aeschines, that you are the city's enemy or mine? Mine, clearly. When it was possible for you to seek legal satisfaction from me, if I committed a crime, for the benefit of these Athenian citizens, in the audits, in civil suits, in the other trials, you neglected to do so. (125) Have you chosen to face me where I am immune in all respects: in respect to the laws, to the time that has passed, to the statute of limitations; immune because the facts of the case have been frequently argued in court, because I have never been convicted of any wrong against you citizens, because the city must have a larger or smaller share with me in the reputation she gained from her actions? Watch out that you don't prove to be the enemy of these citizens here, while you claim to be mine.

(126) Since I have shown you the only vote which respects your oath as well as justice, it seems, because of his calumnies and not because I am fond of abuse, that I must state some bare facts about him, in return for the many lies he has told about me; and I must point out who he is and who his parents were that he can so readily break into abuse and ridicule certain expressions of mine, although he has himself used words—what decent man would not hesitate to give voice to his language—? (127) If Aiakos or Rhadamynthos or Minos were the prosecutor, and not this idle babbler, this court hack, this damned secretary, I think none of them would say what Aeschines says nor provide from his repertoire such offensive expressions, like an actor in a tragedy bawling out "O Earth and Sun and Virtue" and such phrases, and then appealing to "Education and Intelligence, by which noble and ignoble acts are distinguished." You were familiar with his performances, of course. (128) What do you and yours have to do with "Virtue," you scum? How can you distinguish the noble from the ignoble? Where did you get this knowledge? How can you claim it? What right have you to mention "Education"? No one who is truly educated would make any such claim about himself, but would blush even if another claimed it for him. People who have missed out on education, like you, but tactlessly affect it,

make their listeners cringe with pain when they speak, and their pretense fails.

(129) I have no difficulty in finding things to say about you and your family; my difficulty is where to begin. Should I say that your father, Trembler, was a slave in the elementary school of Elpias near the Theseum, wearing leg-irons and a wooden collar? Or that your mother plied her trade of daylight marriages in the little shack near the statue of Kalamites, she who raised you, her pretty little doll, to be the paragon of third-rate actors? Everybody knows this and I don't have to mention it. But should I mention that the boatswain Phormio, the slave of Dion the Phrearrian, raised her out of this noble occupation? By all the gods in heaven, I hesitate to say what deserves to be said about you, lest I be thought to have chosen expressions unworthy of me. (130) I will let that be and begin from the kind of life Aeschines led. He was born of no ordinary parents; they were the type of parents solemnly cursed by the Athenian people. Late in his career—do I say late? It was yesterday or the day before that he became an Athenian citizen and an Athenian politician at the same time. By adding a syllable, he made his father Nontrembler instead of Trembler; his mother was endowed with the quite exalted name, Eyegleam, though everyone knows she was called Hobgoblin, a name derived from her occupation because she would do anything and submit to every request of her clients. How else did she get it? (131) You were elevated from slavery to freedom and from begging to riches thanks to these citizens, but you are such an ingrate and so deformed in your nature that you have no way to thank them except by selling yourself and pursuing a policy detrimental to their interests. I will not mention his speeches; some might claim they were delivered in the city's interest. But I will remind you of his actions; their results have shown that they were clearly in our enemies' interest.

(132) Who among you does not know of the case of Antiphon? He was deprived of his citizenship, but returned to Athens after promising Philip that he would burn the dockyards. I found him hiding in Peiraios and, when I brought him before your Assembly, Aeschines, that malicious man, yelled and screamed that my action was outrageous in a democratic

state, that I was insulting citizens who were down on their luck, that I had entered a home without a supporting order. He obtained Antiphon's release. (133) If the Council of the Areopagus, which learned of the case and saw that your ignorance of the facts was untimely, had not ordered a further investigation, arrested the man and brought him to you for trial, he would have been snatched from your grasp, avoided his penalty, and been sent on his way by this mouther of noble phrases. As it was, you tortured him and put him to death, the penalty which Aeschines should have received. (134) The Council of the Areopagus knew of his activities in that case; and when you elected him to argue your side in the dispute about the Delphic temple, out of the same ignorance of the facts which has caused you to sacrifice many of your interests, the Council, which the Assembly had made its associate and put in control of the matter, rejected him as a traitor and instructed Hypereides to take on the task. Their votes were solemnly placed on the altar, and no vote was cast for this morally polluted man. To prove that I speak the truth, call the witnesses.

WITNESSES (135)

(136) Accordingly, when the Council rejected him as an advocate and chose another, it declared its opinion that he was a traitor and opposed to your interests.

Here was one of the typical acts of this hothead, similar—is it not?—to acts of mine he attacks? Let me remind you of another. When Philip sent Python of Byzantium and a group of ambassadors from each of his allies to put the city to shame by showing her injustice, I did not retreat before the flood of insolent rhetoric which Python spat at you, but I rose and refuted his claims. I did not play false our city's reputation for just dealings, and showed Philip to be in the wrong so convincingly that his own allies rose and agreed with me. But Aeschines here was on Philip's side and asserted that the false and inimical claims of Python were true.

(137) That was not enough. Afterwards, he was caught with Anaxinos, the spy, at Thrason's house. Whoever associates closely with, and makes plans with, an emissary of the enemy

must himself be naturally presumed to be a spy and hostile to his country. To prove that I speak the truth, please summon the witnesses.

WITNESSES

(138) I omit a thousand other things I could say about him. For the situation is like this. I have many more facts to point to, which reveal that he served the enemy in that period and treated me insolently. But you don't have an accurate memory of these facts nor have they aroused the anger they deserve; rather, by a habitual weakness of yours, you have given anyone who wants it a complete license to trip up and falsely accuse him who speaks to your advantage, and you exchange the city's benefit for the joy and pleasure you get from listening to abuse. Consequently, it is always easier for a person to serve the enemy and to take bribes than to serve his city as a patriot.

(139) It was a fearful thing—Earth and the gods, how could it not have been?—to take Philip's side against our country, even before we were openly at war with him. Yet, allow him, if you want, allow him this. But when our ships had been openly seized and robbed, when the Chersonese was being plundered, when the man was marching toward Attica, the situation was no longer in dispute, war was upon us. This evil man, this writer of lampoons, cannot point out anything he did to serve you nor is there any decree in the city's favor, either of large or of small importance, which carries the name of Aeschines. If he says there is, let him specify it; he can use my speaking-time. There is none. One of two things must be the case: either he proposed no measures beyond what I proposed, because he found no fault with what I was doing, or he did not produce better measures, because he was seeking ways to help the enemy.

(140) As he made no proposals, did he also fail to speak, whenever the need to harm you arose? No one else had a chance to speak. Most of his other actions, it seems, the city was able to tolerate, and he was able to get away with them. But one accomplishment caps all his previous ones, men of Athens, and he has spent a lot of time talking about it. I refer to the

details he gave us about the Amphissians' decrees in hope of distorting the truth. In fact, he cannot do it. How could he? You will never wash away the stain of those actions. You don't have enough words.

(141) In your presence, men of Athens, I invoke all the gods and goddesses who protect the land of Attica, and Pythian Apollo, our city's paternal god; if I should be speaking the truth now and spoke the truth before the people as soon as this impious man involved himself in that affair (for I knew it, I knew it immediately), I pray all of them to grant me continued and secure good fortune; but if, because of my hatred of Aeschines and my personal ambition, I am dragging in a false charge against him, I pray them to take away anything good I might have.

(142) Why have I made this solemn prayer and extended it to such lengths? Because, although I have the records which were deposited in the public archives—these will provide clear proof—and know that you will recall what happened, I fear that he may be thought incapable of the crimes he has committed. Indeed, this happened before, when he caused the poor Phocians to be destroyed by reporting false information to Athens. (143) It was Aeschines who assisted Philip in bringing on the war in Amphissa, which enabled Philip to come to Elateia, and a man to be chosen leader of the Amphictyonic Council, who completely overturned the situation in Greece; this one man—Aeschines—is responsible for all the terrible results. When I protested right away and cried in the Assembly, "You are importing a war into Attica, Aeschines, an Amphictyonic war," some—those with whom he had packed the Assembly—would not let me go on speaking, others were surprised and thought that I was bringing an unfounded charge because of my personal hostility toward him. (144) What the true nature of that situation was, why these preparations were made, how their plans were accomplished, hear now, since you were prevented from doing so then. You will see that the plot was well organized; you will get much help for learning about public policies, and you will discern how very clever Philip was.

(145) There was no end to the war against you nor relief for Philip, unless he were to make Thebes and Thessaly hostile

to our city. Although your generals were conducting a sorry and ineffective war against him, he still was suffering many setbacks from pirates and because of the mere fact of the war. He could not export any of the products of his own country nor have imported what he needed.

(146) At that time, he was no stronger than you on sea nor was he able to invade Attica without the help of his Thessalian accomplices and unless the Thebans allowed him passage. When he did begin to win out over whatever kind of generals you sent (I will not speak of these), he was still at a disadvantage because of the nature of the locality and the relative resources of each side. (147) If, to pursue his own hostility, he were to persuade either the Thessalians or the Thebans to march against you, he thought that no one would pay any attention to him. But if he were to find some grounds common to both and were elected their leader, he expected to win out more easily, partly by deception, partly by persuasion. What then? He attempts—how successfully you will see—to involve the Amphictyons in a war and create a disturbance at the meeting in Thermopylæ. He supposed that they would require his immediate leadership for this war. (148) If one of his own Council delegates or one of his allies introduced this matter, he believed that the Thebans and the Thessalians would be suspicious and everybody would be on his guard. But if an Athenian did this, someone sent by you, his enemies, he would easily avoid suspicion. This is what happened. How did he accomplish it? He hired Aeschines. (149) Since no one foresaw this plot, I think, or guarded against it—this is the way things are usually handled by you—Aeschines was nominated Council delegate and was declared elected when three or four hands were raised in his favor. When he came to the meeting of the Council, attended by the prestige of our city, he completely ignored everything else and set about the job for which he was hired. Composing some specious and fanciful tales about why the plain of Kirrha had been consecrated and relating them to men unused to hearing speeches and unable to see what was coming, (150) he persuaded them to vote an inspection of the plain which the Amphissians claimed belonged to them for cultivation but which he alleged was part of the consecrated land. The Amphissians

were bringing no suit against us then nor were they doing what he now falsely claims as his excuse. The proof is here. It was not possible, of course, for the Amphissians to prepare a suit against the city without a summons being served. Who served this summons on us? On what authority? Mention someone who knows, point him out. You cannot; this was an empty and false pretext you used. (151) While the Amphictyons were making a survey of the land according to the directions of Aeschines, the Amphissians attacked and nearly killed all of them; in fact, they seized some of the delegates. Once legal charges and war were stirred up against the Amphissians, at first Kottyphos led an army of Amphictyons; but when some members did not join the expedition, others joined but didn't do anything, those with whom arrangements had been made, the longtime traitors in Thessaly and the other cities, were for putting Philip in charge of the war before the coming meeting in the autumn. (152) And they had specious reasons. Either, they claimed, the members themselves had to contribute to the support of a mercenary army and fine non-contributors, or they had to elect Philip. Need I say more? The result was the election of Philip as leader of the war. Immediately afterwards, he collected a force and started out as if toward Kirrha, but, quite ignoring the Kirrhaians and the Amphissians, he seized Elateia. (153) If the Thebans had not reversed themselves immediately upon seeing this and joined our side, the whole thing would have swept into our city like a river in torrent. As it was, they checked him, for the moment at least, thanks especially, men of Athens, to the good will of one of the gods, but, besides that, thanks to my efforts insofar as it depended on one man. Give me, please, those resolutions and the records of the times at which each of the events took place, so that you may see how much disturbance this evil man caused, without paying the penalty for it. Read the resolutions, please. (154)

RESOLUTION OF THE AMPHICTYONS
SECOND RESOLUTION (155)

Read also the record of the time of these events. They took place when this man was a delegate to the Council.

RECORDS

(156) Give me the letter which Philip sent to his allies in the Peloponnese, when the Thebans would not comply, so that you may learn clearly from this too that he concealed his true reason for action, which was to harm Greece and Thebes and you, and claimed to be doing what was for the common interest and what had been resolved by the Amphictyons. It was Aeschines who provided him with a starting point and a pretext. Read the letter.

LETTER (157)

(158) You see that he avoids any personal motives, but takes refuge in reasons supplied by the Amphictyons. Who assisted him in arranging these circumstances? Who provided him with those reasons? Who is the one most responsible for the trouble which ensued? Is it not Aeschines here? But, men of Athens, do not go around saying that the troubles Greece suffered were caused by a single man, Philip. Not by a single man, but by many evil men in each city, on Earth and the gods. (159) Aeschines was one of them and, if I had to speak the truth without reserve, I would not hesitate to say that he was the accursed plague which caused the loss of everything afterwards, of men, of places, of cities. For it is the sower of the seed who is responsible for the crop of evil. I am surprised that you did not recoil from him as soon as you saw him. But a cloud of darkness, it seems, stands between you and the truth.

(160) Since I have touched upon his actions against our country, I have come around to discussing the policies I chose in opposition to his. There are many reasons why you should hear them from me; the main one is that it is a shameful thing, men of Athens, if, while I endured the actual labors in your behalf, you cannot bear to hear a review of them. (161) When I saw that, under the influence of men in both cities who were sympathetic to, and had been corrupted by, Philip, the Thebans, as well as you to a large extent, were ignoring what should have been a cause of fear to both peoples and were entirely inattentive to what required much and careful atten-

tion, namely that Philip was being permitted to grow powerful and that you were on the point of hostility and an open clash, I was continually on my guard to prevent this. It was not only my own judgment that this was the best policy, (162) but I knew that Aristophon and, after him, Euboulos wanted perpetual friendship between you; I knew also that, while they frequently disagreed on other matters, they were always of the same mind on this. When they were alive, you sly beast, you were their most attentive flatterer, but now you don't see that it is dead men you are accusing. In censuring my Theban policy, you are attacking them more than me, for they approved this alliance before I did. (163) But I return to the main point, that Aeschines caused the war in Amphissa and that Aeschines and his accomplices succeeded in creating hostility against the Thebans. Then Philip marched against you, which was their purpose in setting the cities at odds. If we had not roused ourself a little too soon, we would have been unable to recover. Their plot was that close to success. What your relations were with Thebes at that stage, you will learn from these decrees and the replies to them. Please read them.

DECREE (164)

SECOND DECREE (165)

(166) Read also his replies.

REPLY TO THE ATHENIAN PEOPLE

REPLY TO THE THEBAN PEOPLE (167)

(168) This was how Philip created dissension between the cities, and, encouraged by the decrees and replies, he came with a force and seized Elateia, feeling that it would no longer be possible for us and the Thebans to act in harmony. All of you know the confusion which then beset the city; nevertheless, listen to a few—the most essential—details.

(169) It was evening. Someone came reporting to the Prytanes that Elateia had been captured. Some of them got up immediately, in the middle of dinner, and began to drive out the merchants in the stalls around the market place and to burn the wicker booths; others had the generals summoned and called for the trumpeter. The city was filled with confusion. At

dawn of the next day, the Prytanes summoned the Council to the Council chamber, while you proceeded to the Assembly. The whole people was already seated before the Council started their business and passed a motion. (170) Afterwards, when the Council came and the Prytanes reported the information they had received, they brought in the messenger, and he spoke. Then the herald asked, "Who wishes to speak?" No one came forward. The herald asked the same question again and again, but no one rose, although all the generals were present, all the orators were present, and although our country was calling for someone to speak for its security. For it is right to believe that the voice of the herald, when he speaks as the laws direct, is the common voice of our country. (171) And yet, if we only needed men to come forward who wanted our country secure, all of you, with the rest of the citizens of Athens, would have mounted the speaker's platform. For all of you, I know, wanted Athens to be saved. If we needed the wealthy to come forward, the 300 would have; if we needed men with both these qualifications, patriotism and wealth, those who made large contributions afterwards would have come forward; for this act was motivated by their patriotism and their wealth. (172) But, the crisis of that day, as it seems, called not only for the patriotic and wealthy citizen, but also for a man who had closely followed the course of events from the beginning and who had correctly reasoned why and with what intention Philip was acting. For one who did not know this and who had not carefully examined the situation for a long time, not even if he were patriotic, not even if he were wealthy, was any the more likely to know what had to be done or able to advise you. (173) That man, on that day, was I. I came forward and addressed you, and you should now attentively listen to what I said then, for two reasons: the first, that you may realize that I, alone of the advisers on public policy, did not desert the post that patriotism required in time of danger, but the record shows that I advised and proposed what had to be done for your sake in that fearful crisis; the second, that by spending a little of your time now, you may become far more experienced in the whole area of public policy for the future. (174) I said then, "I think that those who are overly disturbed because they believe that the Thebans are firmly on Philip's side are ignorant of the actual state of affairs. For I am convinced that, if this were so, we would hear, not that he is in Elateia, but that he is at our borders. I am certain, however, that he has come to prepare matters in Thebes. Hear, (I said), why this is so. (175) He has prepared to receive his orders all the Thebans he could bribe or deceive. In no way can he win over those who took a stand against him originally and remain opposed to him now. What is his purpose and why has he seized Elateia? By making a show of force and displaying his armament near their city, he hopes to encourage and embolden his supporters and stun his opposition so that they will either yield through fear what they are now unwilling to or may be compelled to do so. (176) If, in the present situation, we choose to remember any trouble the Thebans caused us in the past and mistrust them because they are now on the enemy side, we will, in the first place, answer Philip's prayers, and I fear also that both Philip and the Thebans will march upon Attica, if we look at all the Thebans, those who oppose him and those who support him, in the same light. But if you accept my advice and look carefully, rather than cavil, at what I am saying, you will agree, I think, that I am advising what must be done and that I will free the city from the danger which hovers over it. (177) What do I propose? First, dismiss the fear you have now; then, turn and fear for the Thebans. They are much nearer disaster than we, and the danger will come upon them first. Secondly, those of military age and the cavalry should march to Eleusis and make it clear to everybody that you are at arms, so that the Thebans who sympathize with us may have an equal chance to speak freely about a just course when they see that, as there is a military force in Elateia to support those who are selling out their country to Philip, so you are at hand ready to help those who want to fight for their freedom, if anyone attacks them. (178) After this, I recommend that you elect ten ambassadors, and give these, with the generals, authority to decide when you should march there and the details of the march itself. How do I suggest that the ambassadors deal with the situation when they arrive at Thebes? Pay close attention to me here. They should not ask the Thebans for a thing (their crisis makes any request shameful) but promise to come to their aid, if they so instruct us, since they are now in extreme danger and we are in a better position to see what will happen than they. If they accept our proposals and advice, we may have accomplished what we wish and have done so with a motive worthy of our city; if it turns out that we fail, they may have themselves to blame for any mistake they make, while no action we took was shameful or mean." (179) With these and similar recommendations, I stepped down. All, together, praised my advice; no one opposed it. I did not speak, but fail to propose measures; I did not propose measures, but fail to serve as ambassador; I did not serve as ambassador, but fail to persuade the Thebans; from beginning to end I persevered and faced, without reserve, the dangers threatening the city. Please read the decree which was voted then.

(180) But wait. Aeschines, how do you wish me to describe your position, and mine, on that day? Was I Battalos, your insulting and degrading nickname for me; were you—no ordinary hero, but one of the great heroes of the stage—Kresphontes or Kreon or Oinomaos, a part which you once murdered in a performance at Kollytos? In that time of crisis, I, Battalos of Paiania, was clearly of more value to his country than you, Oinomaos of Kothokidai. You were entirely useless; I did everything the duty of a good citizen required. Read the decree, please.

DECREE OF DEMOSTHENES (181–187)

(188) This was the beginning and the first step in establishing good relations with Thebes; before this, thanks to the influence of these men, there was hatred and distrust and hostility between the two cities. This decree made the danger then hanging over our city pass by like a cloud. It was the duty of the good citizen, if he had anything better to advise, to bring it into the open then, and not be criticizing my policy now. (189) For the adviser and the malicious opportunist, who are alike in no other way, differ most in this: the one reveals his opinion before the events and makes himself responsible to those he has persuaded, to fortune, to opportunities, to all men; the other, who was silent when he should have spoken, cavils if anything

unpleasant results. (190) Then, as I said, was the opportunity for one who cared about his city and about honest advice. I even go so far as to say that I acted wrongly, if he can point to a better policy now or even if there was anything else at all which could have been done, apart from the policy I recommended. If anyone sees any measure now, which would have been beneficial if acted upon then, I say that it should not have escaped me. But if there is none, if there was none, if none can be mentioned even to this day, what should the statesman have done? Should he not have chosen the best of the possible policies which revealed themselves? (191) This is what I did, when the herald asked: "Who wishes to speak?" not, "Who wishes to bring charges about events of the past?" nor, "Who wishes to guarantee what the future will bring?" In those times of crisis, you sat mute in the assemblies; I rose and spoke. You wouldn't then, tell us now. What advice, which should have been available, or what opportunity for Athens was neglected by me? What alliance, what action was there to which I should rather have persuaded these citizens?

(192) Everyone dismisses the past and no one ever proffers advice about it. It is the future or the present which requires the statesman at his post. At that moment, it seems, some danger was in the future, some was already at hand; consider the policy I chose in the circumstances; don't cavil at the outcome. For the final result of all actions depends upon the will of heaven, but the choice itself reveals the mind of the statesman. (193) Don't blame me for a crime, if it turned out that Philip was victorious in battle; the result here rested with the gods, not with me. Show me that I did not choose everything that was possible according to human calculation, and that my actions were not just and careful and that they did not require almost superhuman strength, or that they were not noble, not worthy of the city, not necessary; show me this, and then accuse me. (194) If the lightning that struck us was too great not only for us but for the rest of Greece as well, what were we to do? It is just as if one were to blame for the shipwreck the owner who has taken every precaution, has equipped his ship with everything he believes will ensure its safety, but then the ship meets with a storm and its tackling weakens or is com-

pletely ruined. But I was not a captain of a ship, one might say (as I was not a general either), nor did I control fate; rather, fate controlled everything. (195) Look at it in this way, Aeschines. If this result was fated, although we had the Thebans fighting with us, what should we have expected if we did not have them as allies, but had let them join Philip—a policy which all the eloquence of Aeschines supported? If so much danger, so much fear surrounded Athens when the battle was three days away from Attica, what should we have expected if we had the same experience somewhere on our own territory? Aren't you aware that one and two and three days allowed us to make a stand, to compose and refresh our forces, and provided much for the security of the city? But if—it is not right to mention something we did not have to suffer, by the good will of one of the gods and because the alliance, which you accuse, provided a shield for the city.

(196) All of this—and it has been much—I intended for you, men of the jury, and for the spectators listening outside; a brief and plain account would have been a sufficient reply to this contemptible man. If the future were clear to you alone, Aeschines, you should have spoken out when the city was deliberating. If you did not foresee the future, you have the same responsibility as others for the same ignorance; and so, why should you accuse me rather than I you? (197) I proved myself so much better a citizen than you in these particular events (I do not yet mention others) that I devoted myself to policies which all thought to be advantageous, not hesitating before, nor considering, any personal danger, while you, who had no better policy than mine (if you had, the Athenians would not have followed mine) and did not make yourself at all useful in implementing this policy, are found to be doing precisely what the worst type of man and worst enemy of the city would do after the matter is finished. Aristratos in Naxos and Aristoleus in Thasos, the outright enemies of our city, are bringing to trial the friends of the Athenians; in Athens, at the same time, Aeschines is accusing Demosthenes. (198) And yet, a person who finds matter for personal glory in the misfortunes of Greece would more justly suffer the penalty of death than be accusing another; a person who was benefited by the same time

of crisis as were the enemies of his city cannot be a patriotic citizen. You prove this from your life, from your actions, from your policies, and from your lack of policy. A measure is being discussed which the Athenians think supports their interests; Aeschines is silent. There was resistance, and something unexpected happened; Aeschines is there, like ruptures and strains which afflict the body when it is stricken by some disease.

(199) Since he concentrates his charges on the outcome of these events, I wish to make a rather paradoxical assertion. Do not be amazed, by Zeus and the gods, if I say something extreme; rather, let everyone examine what I say with good will. If the outcome was entirely clear, and everyone knew about it beforehand, and you were predicting it, Aeschines, shouting at the top of your voice—you who did not utter a word—not even in those circumstances should the city have backed off from its course, if in fact it was concerned for its reputation or its forefathers or the future. (200) As it is, it seems we have failed to achieve our material ends, a result which can happen to all men when the gods so decide. But if Athens had claimed to be the leader of the rest of Greece, and then had backed off from this claim in the face of Philip, she would have been open to the charge that she betrayed all of Greece. If she had yielded to Philip, without a fight, what our forefathers had taken every risk to preserve, who would not have spit upon you, Aeschines? Not on the city, not on me. (201) Events have turned out as they have, and Philip has been chosen absolute master of all Greece; but how could we look visitors to Athens in the face, if others apart from us had made the struggle to prevent this result, especially since our city in former times never chose an ignominious security over danger to gain a noble end. (202) Is there any Greek, any non-Greek, who does not know that Athens could have kept what was hers and received whatever she wanted from the Thebans, from the Spartans, who were even stronger than the Thebans before, and from the king of Persia —and they would have been very glad to give it—if she would do what they commanded and allow another power to be the leader of Greece? (203) For Athenians, however, to make such a choice was not something they had learned from their ancestors nor morally tolerable nor natural; from the beginning of

her history, no one has ever been able to persuade our city
to attach herself to those who are strong, but act unjustly, and
live the secure life of slavery; rather, Athens has continually
fought for and taken risks for first place in honor and reputation throughout this time. (204) You should understand that
these qualities are so lofty and so consistent with your character that you reserve your highest praise for those of your ancestors who followed this course. Rightly so. For who would not
admire the courage of the men who endured leaving their city
and their land and taking to warships to avoid obeying another's orders, who chose Themistocles, the adviser of this action, as general, who stoned Kyrsilos to death (and not only
Kyrsilos; your wives slew his wife as well) because he proposed
submission. (205) The Athenians of that day were not looking
for an adviser or a general who would lead them to become
happy slaves, but they did not even think it right to go on living, if they could not live in freedom. Each of them thought
himself a child not of his parents alone but also of his country.
What is the difference? One who considers himself only a
child of his parents is satisfied to await the natural death which
fate brings; he who is a child of his country as well will be
willing to die not to see her enslaved and will believe that the
insults and dishonor he must suffer in a city of slaves are more
to be feared than death itself.

(206) If I were trying to say that I induced you to feel
sentiments worthy of your ancestors, anyone could criticize me
with justice. In fact, I am showing you that this was your own
choice, and I am pointing out that the city had this spirit before
me, but I do say that I contributed some service in each of the
actions you took, and that Aeschines here, (207) who censures
the whole of this policy and bids you to feel bitterness toward
me because I am the cause of the fearful dangers which befell
the city, hungers to deprive me of this immediate honor and is
robbing you of the praise you deserve for all future time. If you
will condemn Ctesiphon on the grounds that my policies were
not for the best, you will be thought to have made a mistake,
and you will make it appear that the results you suffered were
not due to the harshness of fate. (208) But it cannot, it cannot
be that you made a mistake, men of Athens, in taking upon

yourselves the burden of danger for the freedom and security of all; I swear it by your ancestors in the front lines at Marathon, by those who stood at Plataia, by your naval men at Salamis and Artemisium and by many others who lie in public tombs, good men, all of them, whom the city buried because it thought them worthy of the same honor, not only those of them who were successful and victorious. And justly so. For they all performed the duty expected of brave men, and they accepted whatever fate heaven allotted to them. (209) But now, you abominable clerk, in your desire to rob me of the honor and affection of these jurors, you have been talking about victory trophies and battles and deeds of old; which of them do we need in the present trial? Whose spirit should have inspired me, you third-rate actor, when I approached the speaker's platform to advise our city how to preserve her pre-eminence? His, whose advice would be unworthy of these citizens? They would justly have put me to death. (210) For you should not decide public and private lawsuits, men of Athens, from the same point of view: in the one case, you should examine the business contracts of daily life with reference to specific statutes and facts; in judging public policy, you should keep your eyes on the standards of your ancestors. Each of you, when he accepts his juror's staff and ticket, should realize that he is also inheriting the spirit of the city, if indeed you think that your actions should be worthy of your ancestors when you come to court to decide public cases.

(211) But I have digressed about the deeds of your ancestors, and there are decrees and actions I have omitted. I wish to return to the points I was making before my digression.

On arriving at Thebes, we found there representatives of Philip, of the Thessalians and of his other allies, and discovered that our supporters were in fear, his brashly confident. To show that my statements now are not for my own benefit, read, please, the letter which we ambassadors sent back immediately. (212) The malice of Aeschines is so deep that he claims that the opportunity, and not I, was responsible for anything successful that was done; but he blames me and my luck for everything which turned out otherwise. As it seems, I, the adviser and spokesman, seem to him responsible for none of the actions produced by discussion and deliberation; I alone am responsible for our military and strategic failures. How could a person who makes such a malicious accusation be more coarse or more contemptible? Read the letter.

LETTER

(213) When the Thebans called an assembly, they introduced the others first because of their position as allies. They came forward and delivered their harangues, with much praise of Philip, many accusations against you, and frequent reminders to the Thebans of everything you had ever done against them. In short, their claim was that the Thebans should be grateful for the favors they had received from Philip and should inflict whatever penalty they wished upon you for the wrongs they had suffered, either by allowing Philip and his allies to march through Bœotia against you or by joining them in the invasion of Attica. They showed, as they thought, that, if Thebes followed their counsel, animals and slaves, and other possessions of yours would be moved from Attica to Bœotia, but, if Thebes accepted what they alleged we would say, everything in Bœotia would be ravaged by war. They made many additional claims, all tending to the same end. (214) While I would give my whole life to repeat each detail of the reply we made, yet I fear that, since the crisis is past and you may think that everything which took place has been obliterated as if by a flood, you might believe that a detailed discussion would be an empty pile of words. But hear how we persuaded them and how they answered us. Read this document.

REPLY OF THE THEBANS

(215) After this, they invited your help and summoned you. You marched out, you came to their aid, and—to omit the intervening steps—they received you in such a friendly manner that, with their own cavalry and infantry outside the walls, they took your army into the city and into their homes, among their wives and children and most valuable possessions. On that day, the citizens of Thebes showed all the world three qualities of yours which deserve the highest praise: the first is your bravery, the second your justice, the third your decent

behavior. For in choosing to make the fight with you rather than against you, they judged that you were better and your claims more just than Philip's; by putting in your care what they and all men guard most closely, their wives and children, they revealed their confidence in your behavior. (216) In these areas, men of Athens, their judgment about you was obviously correct. When your army had entered the city, no one, even unjustly, made any complaint about you, so decently did you conduct yourselves. When they lined up alongside you in the first battles, the one at the river and the winter battle, you showed yourselves not only faultless but even admirable for your discipline, your state of preparation, and your zeal. On these grounds you received praise from other peoples, you offered sacrifices and processions to the gods. (217) I would take pleasure in asking Aeschines whether he shared your joy and joined in the sacrifices when they were being conducted and the city was filled with pride and joy and praise or did he sit at home, grieving, lamenting, sulking at our common success? If he is proved to have been there with the rest of us, is not his behavior monstrous, or even sacrilegious, if he invoked the gods as witnesses of the excellence of our policy and now thinks it right that you, who have sworn an oath to the gods, should condemn this policy because it was bad? If he was not there, should he not justly suffer a thousand deaths, because he was aggrieved by what was a cause of joy to the rest of us? Please read these decrees as well.

SACRIFICIAL DECREES

(218) While we were engaged in sacrifices and the Thebans believed that they had been rescued by us, it turned out that we, who, it seemed, would require help as a result of the activities of these traitors, were ourselves helping others because you accepted my recommendations. Further, you will learn from the letters Philip sent to the Peloponnese what reactions he voiced and how confused he was at this turn of events. Please read them so that you may see what was accomplished by my persistence, by the journeys I made, by my labors and by the many decrees which Aeschines ridiculed just now.

(219) And yet, men of Athens, you had many great and

famous advisers before me, the notable Kallistratos, Aristophon, Kephalos, Thrasyboulos, a thousand others. Nevertheless, none of these ever put his whole person entirely at the
service of our city, but if one made proposals, he would not
serve as an envoy; if another was an envoy, he would not make
proposals. Each of them reserved for himself some enjoyment
in leisure as well as some resource to fall back on, if anything
went wrong. (220) What is my point? Someone might ask,
"Were you so superior in forcefulness and enterprise that you
did everything yourself?" I do not say this, but I so thoroughly
persuaded myself that the danger which had the city in its
grasp was great that there did not seem to be any room for
consideration of my personal safety, but one had to be content
if he did what he had to do and omitted nothing. (221) As to
myself, I was persuaded—perhaps senselessly, but nevertheless
I was persuaded—that, in proposing measures, no one would
propose better measures than I, that in acting and in serving as
an ambassador, no one could act or serve more zealously and
more correctly than I. For these reasons, I was at my post in
each of these spheres. Read the letters of Philip.

LETTERS

(222) This was the situation in which my policy put Philip,
Aeschines. This was the language he used now, no longer the
many brash threats against the city. For this I was justly voted
a Crown by these citizens; you were there and did not oppose
the Crown; Diondas, who contested it, did not receive a minimum of the votes. Please read the decrees whose legality was
vindicated and which were not contested by Aeschines.

DECREES

(223) These decrees, men of Athens, have precisely the
same words and syllables as those which Aristonikos proposed
before and Ctesiphon proposes now. Aeschines did not contest
them himself and did not assist anyone else contesting them.
Yet it would have been more reasonable for him to prosecute
Demomeles, their proposer, and Hypereides, than Ctesiphon, if
his present accusations are true. (224) Why? Because it is possible for Ctesiphon to refer to those men and to the decisions of

the courts, to the fact that Aeschines did not accuse them when they made the same proposals as he makes now, to the fact that the laws do not allow further indictments on matters settled judicially, and to many other facts. Had Aeschines prosecuted Demomeles and Hypereides, the matter would have been decided on its own merits, before any precedents existed. (225) But in that case, I think, it would not have been possible for Aeschines to follow his present procedure; he misrepresents the facts by selecting details of many decrees from ancient history which no one knew about before the trial or thought would be mentioned today; he seems to say something to the point by rearranging chronology and substituting false grounds of action for the true ones. (226) This procedure would not have worked, but all arguments would have rested on the truth, the events were recent, you still remembered them and almost had each detail in your grasp. For this reason, avoiding an inquiry into the facts, he has come here believing that you will hold a public speaking contest, as it seems to me, and not a review of my policies, and will make it a trial of eloquence, not of which policy was beneficial to the city.

(227) Then he becomes subtle and says you should ignore the opinion about us you had when you came to court; just as you acquiesce when, thinking that someone has a surplus, you total up the accounts and find that both sides of the ledger are even and there is no surplus, so also now you should acquiesce in the plausible conclusions of his argument. But look how rotten, it seems, are the foundations supporting every plan unjustly contrived. (228) By using the clever illustration just mentioned, he has agreed that you must now be assumed to have made a decision about us, that I speak for my country, and he speaks for Philip; he would not be seeking to change your minds, unless such a decision about each of us is to be assumed. (229) Moreover, I will easily show that, in asking you to change this opinion, his statements are unjust; I will do it not by bookkeeping (this type of reckoning is irrelevant to affairs of state) but by reminding you briefly of each detail, using you, my audience, as examiners and witnesses at the same time. Instead of the Thebans joining Philip in an invasion of our land, as all expected, my policy, which Aeschines attacks, caused the

Thebans to line up with you to check Philip; (230) instead of
the war being fought in Attica, it was fought eighty miles from
the city at the farther borders of Bœotia; instead of pirates from
Eubœa plundering and pillaging, the side of Attica on the sea
enjoyed peace throughout the war; instead of Philip seizing
Byzantium and holding the Hellespont, the Byzantines fought
with us against him. (231) Do you think, Aeschines, that the
examination of these results is like bookkeeping? Or should we
erase my services from the books, and fail to consider that they
will be remembered for all time? I do not add, as a credit, that
it was the misfortune of others to suffer that savagery which
Philip displayed once he had people entirely in his power, while
it was our good fortune to reap the fruits of the clemency in
which he draped himself as he schemed for the future. But I
pass over this.

(232) Further, I will not hesitate to say that one who
wishes to examine the record of a statesman fairly, and not
maliciously, would not use the kind of accusations you have
just voiced, inventing illustrations, imitating my words and gestures (the fate of the Greek world, to be sure, depended on
whether I used this word and not that, or moved my hand this
way and not that way) (233) but he would inquire, on the
basis of the facts, what means or military resources our city had
when I entered public life, what resources I gained for her afterwards through my leadership, and what was the condition of
our enemies. If I diminished our power, he would show that
the wrong rested with me; but if I greatly increased it, he
would not bring malicious charges. Since you have avoided this
course, I will take it, and look to see, men of Athens, if my
assertions be fair.

(234) In military resources, the city had the islanders, not
all but the weakest, for Khios, Rhodes, and Corcyra were not
with us. The financial subscription was forty-five talents, and
this had been collected in advance. We had no infantry or cavalry except our citizen forces. What was most frightening of all
and most helpful to the enemy, these traitors had brought all
our neighbors, Megara, Thebes, and Euboea, closer to enmity
than to friendship with us. (235) This was all the city could
rely on, and no one can mention any other resource. Consider

the condition of Philip, whom we were fighting. First, he had absolute rule over his followers, which is the greatest single advantage in war. Second, his followers were armed for war all the time. Third, he was well supplied with money, and did whatever he decided, not publishing his decisions in decrees, not being constantly brought to court by malicious accusers, not defending himself against charges of illegality, not accountable to anyone, but simply ruler, leader, master of all. (236) When I took my position against him (for it is fair to examine this), of what was I master? Of nothing. For even the opportunity to speak on policy, the only privilege I had—and a shared one, at that—you extended equally to Philip's hirelings and to me, and, as often as they got the better of me (these instances were many, whatever reason there was for each of them), that often did you leave the Assembly with your enemies' advantage the result of your deliberations. (237) Although I started with disadvantages like these, I brought into alliance with you Euboea, Akhaia, Corinth, Thebes, Megara, Leukas, Corcyra, and these contributed a total of 15,000 mercenaries and 2,000 cavalry apart from their citizen armies. I effected the largest contribution of money I could. (238) If you talk about the justice of our arrangements with Thebes, Aeschines, or with Byzantium or with Euboea or about equal contributions in general, in the first place you show your ignorance of the fact that once before our city provided 200 of those famous 300 warships which fought for Greece, and did not believe itself cheated, did not put the advisers of this policy on trial, did not take offense at this burden (that would have been shameful) but was grateful to the gods that Athens contributed twice as much as the rest to secure all of Greece from the danger which threatened it. (239) In the second place, it is an empty favor you do these citizens by slandering me. Why is it now you say what I should have done, why did you not offer proposals then, since you were in Athens and were present at the meeting of the Assembly, if indeed proposals were feasible in a time of crisis when we had to accept what circumstances allowed, not what we wished? For there was one man bidding against us and ready to accept immediately the men we drove out of our city and to pay them as well.

(240) But if I am now open to criticism for my actions, what do you think these impious men would say or do, if the cities left us and attached themselves to Philip because I was quibbling about the terms of alliance, and Philip gained control of Euboea and Thebes and Byzantium at the same time? (241) Would they not say that these cities had been given up? That they had been rejected, although they wanted to join you? They would say, "Because of Byzantium, Philip has gained control of the Hellespont, and of the grain route to Greece; because of Thebes, a war between neighbors has shifted its severe burden to Attica; because of pirates with their base in Euboea, the sea has become unsafe." Would they not say this and much more besides? (242) A worthless thing, men of Athens, a worthless thing is a person who brings malicious accusations always and everywhere, a spiteful thing, a fault-finder. This paltry man is an animal to the core, who has done nothing helpful or worthy of a free man from his birth; he is a stage monkey, a rustic Oinomaos, a counterfeit statesman. How has your eloquence helped our country? (243) Why do you speak to us now of the past? You act like a doctor who, when he visits his sick patients, does not prescribe anything to cure them of their sickness, but when one of his patients dies and funeral services are being held, follows the body to the tomb, saying, "If the man had done this and that, he would not have died." Madman, is it now you speak?

(244) If you exult at the defeat to our city which you should lament, accursed man, you will not find that it resulted from anything in my control. Look at it in this way. Wherever you sent me as ambassador, I never came back worsted by Philip's ambassadors, not from Thessaly or Ambracia, not from the Illyrians or from the kings of Thrace, not from Byzantium, not from anywhere else, not, finally, from Thebes, but wherever his ambassadors were defeated in debate, he came in with his weapons and overturned the decision. Do you make me accountable for this, (245) and feel no shame at ridiculing the same man for his cowardice, while claiming that this one man should have been stronger than the whole might of Philip? With words my only weapon? What else did I control? Not the life, not the fate of the soldiers, not the generalship, which you

demand that I justify; that is how stupid you are. (246) Make a complete review of everything for which the statesman is accountable; I do not avoid it. What would this be? To see situations as they arise and to inform the rest of the citizens. This I did. To confine within the smallest possible limits, whenever they arise, hesitation, reluctance to act, ignorance, personal ambition—those necessary and inherent defects of all free governments—and to convert these qualities into concord and friendship and the impulse to do what must be done. All of this I did, and no one will ever find anything left undone, so far as it rested with me. (247) If it should be asked how Philip managed most of what he accomplished, everyone would mention his army and his bribes and his corruption of men in political life. I had no forces at my command or under my control, so that the question of what was done in this sphere does not concern me. In the matter of bribery and corruption, I was victor over Philip. For, as the offerer of a bribe is victor over the taker, if it is accepted, so he who does not take the bribe is victor over the offerer. Thus, our city was not defeated, insofar as I am representative of it.

(248) It was these activities, and many others like them, which I provided to justify Ctesiphon's proposal in my honor; I will now mention what all of you provided. Immediately after the battle, the Athenian people, which knew and had witnessed all my actions, although it was in the middle of a terrible and fearful crisis when it was not surprising that most people would be out of sympathy with me, first voted to approve my suggestions for the security of the city and put into operation, through my decrees, everything which was done for its protection: the posting of guards, the ditches, the expenditures to fortify the city walls. Next, the people chose me from all the citizens in the election of a grain commissioner. (249) Afterwards, when those whose concern it was to injure me banded together and instituted all sorts of suits and trials and impeachments against me, not in their own names at first but using persons who they thought would be quite unknown to you (you know, of course, and remember that I was in court on trial on every day of that first period and these men left nothing untried against me, not the desperation of Sosikles, not the maliciousness of Philokra-

tes, not the madness of Diondas and Malantos) but in all these trials I was safely acquitted, thanks mainly to the gods but also through you and the rest of the citizens of Athens. And justly, for acquittal was in accordance with the truth and to the credit of jurors who rendered the only decision in keeping with the oath they had sworn. (250) In the trials of impeachment, when you voted to acquit me and did not give the minimum vote to the prosecutors, you voted that I acted in the best way; in trials of illegality, I was proved to advise and propose only legal measures; in trials when you put an official seal on my accounts, you further acknowledged that everything I handled was handled fairly and without a suspicion of venality. What name was it proper or right for Ctesiphon to attach to results effected by me? Was it not the name which he saw the Athenian people attach, which he saw the sworn jurors attach, which he saw the truth establish to the world?

(251) "Yes," he says, "but it is Kephalos' glory that he was never brought to trial." Yes, indeed, and a blessed stroke of fortune. But why should a man, who has often been prosecuted but never convicted of any crime, be subject in justice to any greater censure because of that? And yet, men of Athens, as far as Aeschines is concerned, I can claim Kephalos' glory, for he never indicted me or prosecuted me, and so he himself agrees that I am not a worse citizen than Kephalos.

(252) One might see his insensitivity and his spitefulness in every paragraph of his remarks, not least in what he had to say about luck. In general, I think, a man who, only a man himself, criticizes another man for his luck is crazy. For what right does a man, who thinks he is very fortunate and has excellent luck, yet does not know if his luck will last till evening, have to talk about his own luck or reproach another man for his. Since Aeschines, besides much else, has used very arrogant language about this subject, you should watch, men of Athens, how much more truthful and more humane will be my remarks on luck. (253) I believe that the luck of our city is good—and I see that the oracle of Zeus at Dodona declares this to you—but that the luck which now prevails for mankind in general is hard and cruel. What Greek, what non-Greek, has not experienced many evils in these times? (254) I count it part of the good

luck of our city that it chose the noblest course of action and fares better than those Greeks who thought they would live in blessed prosperity by abandoning us. Our disaster and the fact that everything did not turn out as we wished is, I believe, our share of the luck of the rest of mankind. (255) I think an examination of one's personal luck, my own and that of each one of us, should be restricted to his private affairs. This is what I believe about luck, a correct and fair judgment, it seems to me, and to you also, I think. Aeschines says that my own luck is more decisive than the luck of the whole city, that something small and insignificant is more decisive than something excellent and great. How is this possible?

(256) If you wish to examine my luck fully, Aeschines, compare it with your own; and if you find mine to be better than yours, stop reviling it. Compare them from the beginning. And, by Zeus, let no one condemn me for lack of feeling. I don't think a person has sense if he reproaches someone for his poverty or if he prides himself on being raised in wealth. But I am compelled by the cruel and malicious insults of this abusive man to mention things like this, although I will be as moderate as circumstances permit.

(257) When I was a boy, Aeschines, I was privileged to attend the proper schools and my financial advantages were such that I was not compelled to do anything shameful through need; when I left boyhood, my actions were consistent with my antecedents—I was choregus, trierarch, a financial contributor to the city, I was deficient in no area of private or public munificence but was useful to my city and to my friends; when I decided to enter public life, I chose the type of policies which brought me frequent crowns of honor from my own country and from other Greeks, such policies which not even you, my enemies, dare to say were dishonorable. (258) This is the good luck I have enjoyed in my life and, although I could mention many other aspects of it, I pass over them to avoid offending any of you by magnifying myself. You, Aeschines, a man haughty and contemptuous of others, compare your luck with mine, luck which saw you raised in deepest poverty, assisting your father in the schoolroom, grinding ink, swabbing benches, sweeping the room, doing the chores of a servant, not of a free

man's son; (259) when you became a man, you read the holy books for your mother's rituals and organized the other details: at night wearing a fawn skin, mixing the wine, cleansing the initiates by wiping them with mud and bran, and, after the purification, instructing them to say, "I have escaped the bad, I have found the better," priding yourself that no one ever could howl as loudly as you (and I believe it; (260) don't think that he can speak so loudly here without being absolutely brilliant at howling); in the daytime, you led your noble bands through the streets wearing garlands of fennel and poplar, squeezing puffed-cheeked adders and waving them over your head, crying "Euoi Saboi" and dancing to the rhythm of "Hyes Attes Attes Hyes," the leader of the dance, the ivy-wreathed leader of the band, the bearer of the winnowing-fan, and addressed with these titles by the little old ladies, taking your pay in the form of sops and cakes and pastry (what glorious rewards! who would not think himself and his luck most truly blessed to receive them?); (261) when you were enrolled in your deme by some trick (I won't go into that), when you were enrolled, you immediately chose the most honorable of professions, that of a clerk and a flunky to minor officials. When you somehow escaped this career, after committing in it all those acts which you accuse in others, (262) you brought no shame, by Zeus, on any of your former occupations by your life afterwards, but hired yourself out to the actors Simukas and Sokrates, the famous "Groaners," and played your small roles collecting from the audience, like a fruit seller from other people's farms, figs and grapes and olives, getting more from this source than from your dramatic contests, in which your troupe engaged at the risk of its life. For there was a truceless and never-ending war between you and the spectators, who inflicted upon you so many wounds that you naturally ridicule as cowards those who never faced such risks. (263) But, passing over actions which one can attribute to poverty, I will proceed to faults in his way of life which deserve accusation. When somehow it occurred to you to enter public life, you chose the kind of policy which, when our country enjoyed success, made you lead the life of a rabbit, fearing, trembling, always expecting people to strike you for the crimes you knew you were guilty of, but put on a show of boldness when the rest of us had unfortunate luck. (264) What is the just reward a man should get from those living, when his spirit is emboldened by the death of a thousand citizens? I omit many other details about his character. For it is not every ugly and shameful reproach which attaches itself to him that I can scrupulously mention, but only those whose mention brings no disgrace to me.

(265) Compare the kind of lives each of us lived, calmly, Aeschines, not bitterly. Then ask these jurors whose luck each of them would choose. You taught school, I attended school. You initiated people, I was an initiate. You were a minor clerk, I was a member of the Assembly. You were a minor actor, I was a spectator. You were hissed off the stage, I joined in the hissing. Your policies supported our enemy, mine, our country. (266) I pass over the rest, but now, today, my qualifications to receive a Crown of honor are under examination, it is agreed that I have done no wrong; the reputation you have as a malicious accuser is set, you are in constant danger, whether you must continue to behave like this or whether you will soon be stopped, by failing to receive a minimum of the votes. Good luck has marked your life—good, indeed!—and you accuse my luck.

(267) Bring here the evidence which deals with my voluntary services and let me read them to you. Alongside these, Aeschines, you read the verses you murdered, "I am come to the crypt of the dead and the gates of darkness" and "Be assured I have no wish to bring evil tidings" and "evil man, evilly" may you be destroyed, first by the gods and then by all of these jurors, bad citizen and bad actor alike.

Read the evidence.

EVIDENCE

(268) This is the way I was in public matters. In my private life,—if all of you do not know that I was at the service of all, humane and generous to those in need, I am silent; I would not mention a thing; I would not even provide evidence for my actions, whether ransoming some citizens from the enemy, whether assisting others with dowries for their daughters, nothing like this. (269) For I have this conviction. I believe that

one who receives a favor should remember it all his life, but
that he who does the favor should put it out of his mind immediately, if he is to behave like a man of honor, not of mean
spirit. To be reminding people and to keep talking about one's
personal favors is nearly the same as reproaching them. I will
do nothing like this, nor will I be induced to, it is enough for
me that you know how I feel in such matters.

(270) Leaving the topic of my private life, I wish to add a
few remarks about political matters. If you can say, Aeschines,
that there is any man under the sun, Greek or non-Greek, who
has escaped harm from the tyranny of Philip before, and of
Alexander now, all right, I grant that my—whether you prefer
to call it luck or bad luck—has been entirely responsible. (271)
But if many, who never saw me or heard my voice, have
suffered many and harsh troubles—not only individuals but
also whole cities and peoples—how much truer and fairer is it
to believe that the general luck, as it seems, of all mankind and
the cruel and inescapable rush of events is responsible. (272)
You dismiss this and blame me, whose political career has been
spent among these citizens, although you know that part at
least, if not the whole, of your abuse falls upon all the citizens
and especially upon you. For if I had absolute control of our
deliberations in my hands, it would be possible for you other
speakers to blame me. (273) But if you were at all the meet-
ings of the Assembly, on each occasion when the city put forward for consideration the question of correct policy, and if my
policies seemed to all to be the best, and especially to you,
Aeschines (for it was not out of good will toward me that you
yielded your hopes for the pride and honor which attended the
results produced through me, but clearly you were defeated by
the truth and had nothing better to advise), how can your
words fail to be unjust, fail to be cruel, when you now censure
these citizens for policies you could not improve on then?
(274) I see that certain principles are defined and settled by all
men in this way. A man commits a crime voluntarily; the result
is anger and punishment of him; a man made a mistake invol-
untarily; punishment is replaced by sympathy. A man commits
no crime, makes no mistake, devotes himself entirely to a policy
which all think beneficial but, in common with all, fails of suc-

cess; it is not just to reproach or revile such a man, it is just to share his grief. (275) Not only will all these principles appear in our laws, but nature itself has defined them in unwritten laws and in the customs of mankind. Aeschines has so surpassed all men in malicious savagery that he blames me for what he himself has called the results of bad luck.

(276) Besides this, as if all his words were straightforward and patriotic, he told you to watch me and be careful that I didn't confuse or deceive you, calling me eloquent, a magician with words, a sophist, and similar epithets, assuming that the fact that he attributes his own qualities to me first will make it so and that his audience will not further consider who is making these statements. I am sure that all of you know him well and believe that these qualities belong much more to him than to me. (277) And I am sure that my skill as a speaker—granted that I have it. Yet I see that the audience has the most control over the impression speakers make. For the way that you listen and the amount of goodwill you have toward each speaker determines your opinion of his wisdom. If I do have a skill of this sort, you will find that, in public matters, it is ranged always on your side, never against you nor for private profit; conversely, Aeschines' skill is used not only to help our enemies, but also against people who might have caused him some trouble or crossed him in some way. He does not use it for just causes or for the city's advantage. (278) The respectable and honorable citizen should not ask jurors who have come here to judge matters affecting the whole city to confirm his anger or hostility or any similar feeling, nor should he appear before you for this purpose but, best of all, these feelings should not be part of his nature; if he must have them, they should be mild and moderate. In what instances should the political speaker be vehement? When one of the vital interests of the city is at stake, and when the city has to deal with its opponents. These are the concern of the honorable and good citizen. (279) But for a person, who has never demanded that you inflict a penalty on me for any public crime—I will add, nor for a private offense— to satisfy the city or to satisfy himself, to come here concocting accusations against a motion to crown and praise me is the mark of personal enmity, of spite, of a mean spirit, not of a

worthwhile citizen. To go further and, dismissing the chance of suits against me, to attack Ctesiphon is the ultimate in worthlessness. (280) With this approach, Aeschines, you seem to me to have chosen to make this a contest of eloquence and of declamation, not to demand punishment for any crime. The language of the speaker, Aeschines, is not a valuable thing, nor the pitch of his voice; it is to choose the same policy as the people, to hate and admire the same persons his country does. (281) One with such a spirit will say everything he says with patriotism his guide; he who courts those from whom the city sees some danger to itself does not ride at the same anchor with the people and cannot have the same expectation of safety. But, don't you see, I can. I chose to act in the interests of these citizens and had no separate or personal interest. (282) Can the same be said of you? How could it be? Immediately after the battle, you went as envoy to Philip, who was responsible for the disasters that those days brought upon your country, although, as everybody knows, you persistently denied any connection with him before that. Yet, who is the one who deceives his city? Is it not he who does not say what is in his mind? Is it not he upon whom the herald lays a solemn and just curse? Is it not a man like Aeschines? What greater crime can be imputed to a political speaker than that what he says and what he feels are two different things? This was found to be true of you. (283) Can you still speak, do you still dare to look these jurors in the face? Do you think they don't know who you are? Or do you think they are so sleepy and so forgetful that they do not remember the speeches you made in the Assembly in the course of the war, solemnly avowing and swearing on oath that there was nothing between you and Philip, but that I was charging you with this because of my own hostility toward you and knew that the charge was untrue. (284) As soon as the result of the battle was reported, you owned up to it immediately, unconcerned with what you said before, and claimed that you were his friend and his guest, substituting "friend" for "hireling." What claim of equality could justify any relationship which makes Aeschines, the son of Eyegleam, the drum-beater, the guest or friend or even acquaintance of Philip? I see none, but the fact is that you sold yourself to pervert the interests of these citizens. In spite of this, Aeschines, although you are caught by the evidence which shows you to be a traitor and have so testified against yourself after the events, you insult and abuse me for results for which you will find everyone else more responsible than me.

(285) Our city, through the policies advocated by me, Aeschines, has had many great and glorious successes, which it has not forgotten. For when the Athenian people were electing a speaker to deliver the eulogy over the dead at the very time of these events, they did not elect you when you were nominated, although you had a fine voice, nor Demades, who had just negotiated the peace, nor Hegemon, nor any other of your friends; they elected me. And when you and Pythokles came forward like savage and ruthless animals, by Zeus and the gods, and made the same abusive accusations which you are making now, the people voted for me all the more eagerly. (286) You are not unaware of the reason, but I will tell you anyway. For the people knew our two qualities, the patriotic zeal which directed my actions, and your injustice. For you and your accomplices admitted, when the city was defeated, what you had denied on oath, when its fortunes were flourishing. The people realized that those who spoke their minds with an impunity gained from the disaster we suffered had been their enemies long before, but then were clearly proved so. (287) They thought it proper that the eulogist who was to adorn the courage of their dead not be under the same roof with nor share the same sacrificial ritual with those who had fought against our dead; that he should not revel in Philip's camp, singing songs of victory at the disaster to Greece in the company of the murderers and then come here to receive distinction; that he should not lament their fate like an actor with tears in his voice, but share our grief in his heart. They saw these qualities in themselves and in me, not in you. (288) This is the reason they elected me and not you. Nor was it the case that the fathers and brothers of the dead, who were chosen by the people to arrange the burial, felt any differently, but, when it came time for them to hold the funeral banquet at the home of the person who was closest to the dead, as is the custom at public funerals, they held it at my home. And with reason. For while one indi-

vidual was closer to another by reason of birth, no one was closer than I to them all together. The man who was most concerned with their safety and success was the one who had the largest share of grief at the lamentable fate of them all.

(289) Read for him the epigram which the city selected to be inscribed at public expense at their graves, so that you may realize, Aeschines, how pitiless, how malign, how disgusting even this epigram shows you to be.

EPIGRAM

(290) Do you hear, Aeschines? "Never to fail, always to succeed, is a privilege of the gods." It is not to the adviser, but to the gods, that the poet attributes the power to guarantee the success of soldiers in combat. Why then, accursed man, do you abuse me with this charge and make remarks which I pray the gods to turn upon the heads of you and your accomplices.

(291) Aeschines has made many other false accusations, men of Athens, but I was especially surprised that, when he was mentioning the catastrophes to our city, his attitude was not that of a patriotic and just citizen, he shed no tear, he felt no such emotion in his heart; but he shouted and roared and strained his voice, quite clearly thinking that he was accusing me but in fact producing evidence to his own discredit and proving that he did not share the feelings of the rest of us at these distressing events. (292) Yet one who claims, as he does, to be concerned for our laws and our constitution, must have this quality at least, if no other, that he shares the same grief and the same joy as the majority of his fellow citizens, and must not, in matters of public policy, be lined up on the side of their opponents. The purpose of what you have now been doing is obvious: you claim that I am to blame for everything and that the city met with its troubles because of me, since it was not from my policy that you citizens began to send assistance to other Greeks. (293) For if you concede that it was through my influence that you opposed Philip's rising dominion over Greece, you would be granting me a gift greater than all the gifts you have ever bestowed on others. But I would not say this (for I would be doing you an injustice) nor, I know, would you concede it. If Aeschines were acting fairly, he would never

damage and disparage the greatest of your glories, because of his hostility toward me.

(294) But why do I object to this behavior, when he has attacked me with far more shocking lies? If he accuses me, for heaven's sake, of Philippizing, what would he shrink from saying? Yet, by Herakles and all the gods, if you should look at the truth of it, discarding his lies and any statements motivated by his hostility, and ask who really were the men to whom all would reasonably and fairly attach the blame for what has happened, you would find that they were the men in each city like Aeschines, not like me. (295) When Philip's power was small and quite insignificant and we were constantly warning and urging and advising excellent policies, it was these who, with their shameful desire for personal profit, sacrificed the common interest, each deceiving and corrupting his fellow-citizens until he enslaved them: in Thessaly, Daokhos, Kineas, Thrasydaos; in Arkadia, Kerkidas, Hieronymos, Eukampidas; in Argos, Myrtis, Teledamos, Mnaseas; in Elis, Euxitheos, Kleotimos, Aristaikhmos; in Messene, Neon and Thrasylokhos, the sons of that damned Philiades; in Sikyon, Aristratos, Epikhares; in Corinth, Deinarkhos, Demaretos; in Megara, Ptoiodoros, Helixos, Perillos; in Thebes, Timolaos, Theogeiton, Anemoitas; in Euboea, Hipparkhos, Kleitarkhos, Sosistratos. (296) The day will not be long enough for me to list the names of the traitors. All of these, men of Athens, had the same purposes in their own countries as Aeschines and his associates here, fawning flatterers of Philip and polluted with a guilt that cries for vengeance; each of them crippled his own country, sacrificed its freedom, first to Philip, now to Alexander, measured happiness by his belly and his ugly desires, and subverted the standards of freedom and rejection of tyranny, which to Greeks before were the prime criteria for success.

(297) As a result of my policies, our city is guiltless in the eyes of all mankind and I am guiltless in your eyes of this shameful and notorious conspiracy of evil—or rather, to speak precisely, of betrayal of the freedom of Greece. Do you then ask me, Aeschines, for what special excellence I claim to deserve honor? I say to you that, when all the political leaders in Greece, beginning with you, had been corrupted, (298) no op-

portunity, no courteous language, no large promises, no hope, no fear, nothing inspired or induced me to betray any of the interests, which, in my judgment, were proper and good for Athens. Unlike your group, none of the advice I gave these citizens was weighed, as on a scale, to my own profit, but was given with correct, just, and uncorrupted motives. More than any of my contemporaries I took charge of important affairs and handled them fairly and beneficially. For this I claim to deserve honor. (299) The fortification of the walls, my part in which you ridiculed, and the trenchworks deserve, in my judgment, gratitude and praise. Why shouldn't they? But I put them near the bottom of the list of my political achievements. It was not with stone or brick alone that I fortified this city, nor did I think this the greatest of my acts. But if you wish to examine the protective measures I took fairly, Aeschines, you will find weapons and cities and places and harbors and ships and horses and men for their defense. (300) This was the shield I put in front of Attica, as much as was possible by human calculation, and this is how I fortified our land, not with a wall around the Peiraios or around the city. I was not defeated by the calculations of Philip, far from it, nor by his preparations; but the generals of our allies and their forces were defeated by fate. What are the proofs of this? They are clear and obvious. Consider them.

(301) What was the duty of the patriotic citizen, what the duty of the man whose action for his country was based on forethought, zeal, and justice? Was it not to gain Euboea for Attica as a shield against attack from the sea, to gain Boeotia against attack from the plains, to gain the states on our southwestern borders against attack from places in the Peloponnese? Was it not to ensure that provisions of grain would be shipped along friendly coasts until they reached Peiraios? (302) Was it not to secure some of these areas, Prokonnesos, the Chersonese, Tenedos, by sending troops to help them and by advising and proposing such measures; to make other areas, Byzantium, Abydos, Euboea, dependable friends and allies? Was it not to cut off the principal resources of the enemy and to supply resources which Athens lacked? All of these measures were brought to fulfillment by my decrees and my policies; (303) if

one wishes to examine them without spite, men of Athens, he will find that they were planned with precision and properly executed and that I did not neglect or ignore or let slip the opportunity to act on each of them; so far as was within the power and the calculation of one man, I left nothing undone. If some divine force, or fate, or the weakness of the generals, or the evil of you who betrayed the cities, or all of these together damaged our whole effort, until it finally was ruined, for what wrong can Demosthenes be blamed? (304) If there had been one man in each of the Greek states who took the same position in the struggle as I did in Athens, or, rather, if Thessaly had provided only one man, if Arkadia had provided one man who had the same sentiments as I, none of the Greeks on this side of Thermopylae or beyond Thermopylae would be in their present trouble (305) but all of them would now be living happily in their own countries, in freedom and autonomy, with complete security and safety, with gratitude for their many blessings to you and to the rest of the Athenian people, because of my efforts. To show you that my words do not adequately describe the results I achieved, since I wish to avoid causing envy, read, please, the list of military expeditions we sent according to my decrees.

LIST OF MILITARY EXPEDITIONS

(306) These and similar actions were the duty of the honorable citizen, Aeschines; if their results had been successful, we would have been without doubt—and, I may add, with justice—pre-eminently great, and, although their results have been different, we have at least a good reputation and the consolation that nobody censures our city or its policy but all blame the fate which determined events to that result. (307) It was, by Zeus, no one's duty to abandon the interests of the city and sell himself to its opponents, to attend to opportunities favorable to the enemy rather than to his own country, to abuse the man who took it upon himself to advise and propose measures worthy of our city and to persevere in them, to watch and remember any harm done to him personally, and to withdraw from public life, as you frequently do, only to remain in the background like a festering sore. (308) There is indeed a kind

of political inactivity, which is proper and helpful to the state and which most of you citizens enjoy honestly. That is not his inactivity, far from it. He withdraws when it pleases him (and it pleases him often) but watches for an occasion when you have had your fill of your constant adviser or fate causes some reverse or something else unpleasant happens (there are many such occasions in human affairs): that is the time for him to appear on the political scene like a sudden wind, with well-trained voice and a repertoire of words and phrases which he cleverly strings together without catching his breath; but these don't provide any help or any good result, they bring only disaster to each of the citizens and disgrace to all. (309) Yet if this training and practice in speaking were based on the proper motives and had the good of the country as its purpose, it should have produced fruits which were good and honorable and helpful to all the citizens, alliances with other cities, sources of revenue, commercial rights, helpful legislation, obstacles to our declared enemies. (310) Athens searched for all of these in the past, and time provided many such opportunities to the honorable man, but you won't appear on the list of honorable men, not first, not second, not third, not fourth, not fifth, not sixth, nowhere, for services which strengthened our country. (311) What alliance did you negotiate for Athens? What help did Athens receive, what good will or glory did it gain? What embassy, what service of yours brought the city greater honor? What success in internal policy or in Greek Policy or in foreign policy was achieved under your leadership? What warships did you provide? What weapons? What dockyards? What fortifications? What cavalry? Of what use were you in anything? What public financial aid did you provide for rich or poor? None. (312) But, my friend, if none of these, at least you offered patriotic zeal. Where? When? You are the worst of all citizens; not even when all the speakers who had ever used the platform contributed for the city's security and, finally, Aristonikos contributed the money his friends had collected to restore his civic rights, not even then did you come forward and contribute a thing. It was not because you were poor. How could it be? You inherited more than five talents from the estate of Philon, your brother-in-law, and the leaders of the symmories made you a gift of two talents to wreck the trierarchic law. (313) But I won't mention that story, to avoid diverting myself from the topic before us by speaking of one thing after another. It is obvious that your failure to contribute was not caused by poverty; you guarded against any act of opposition to those who were the beneficiaries of all your political acts. What were the occasions on which you showed your vigor and your brilliance? When it was necessary to speak to the detriment of the people, then you were most brilliant of voice, and had memorized your part well, an excellent actor, a tragic Theokrines.

(314) You do well to remind us of the men who proved to be great in the past. However, men of Athens, it is not right for him to take advantage of the good will you have toward the dead and in comparison to them to examine me, who am still living among you. (315) Who does not know that all living men are more or less exposed to envy, but that no one, not even an enemy, continues to hate the dead? Since this is a fact of human nature, am I now to be judged or compared with those before me? No. It is neither fair nor equitable; it is fair, Aeschines, to compare me with you or with any other living person who shared your policies. (316) Consider this point, also. Is it better or more honorable for Athens to expose to ingratitude and abuse services to the present generation because of the existence of the immeasurably great services of the men of the past, or should all who act with patriotism share the honor and affection of these citizens? (317) And if it is I who must say it, my political policy, if examined, will prove to resemble and to have the same purposes as the policies of men who were praised in the past, while your policy, Aeschines, is like that of the people who maliciously attacked such men. For it is clear that there were people then who ridiculed contemporary statesmen while praising their predecessors, doing the same spiteful thing as you. (318) Do you now say that I am not at all like the men of the past? Are you, Aeschines? Is your brother? Is any other politician of the present day? I say there is no one. Compare a living man with the living, my good fellow (to use no other name for you) and with his competitors, as we do in all other cases, poets with poets, choruses with choruses, athletes with athletes. (319) Philammon did not

leave Olympia without a Crown because he was inferior to Glaukos of Karystos and other athletes before his own time, but he was crowned and proclaimed victor because he fought best of those who competed against him. And compare me with speakers of our own day, with yourself, with anyone you wish. I do not shrink from being compared with anyone. (320) When our city was free to choose the best policy and a prize for patriotism was open to all, I advised the strongest measures and all our affairs were conducted by my decrees and laws and embassies; no one of your group was anywhere to be seen except when you felt a need to discredit my proposals. But when that unfortunate defeat was suffered, and there was a call no longer for advisers but for men who would submit to orders, who were ready to harm their country for pay, who were willing to court another, then you and each of your comrades were at your post, fine, important people with handsome stallions. I was powerless, I admit it, but I was more patriotic than you.

(321) The well-meaning citizen (to speak about myself in this way cannot cause envy) must have two qualities, men of Athens: when he is in authority, he should persist in the policy which aims at the city's pre-eminence and honor, but at every time and in every action, he should be patriotic. For his nature controls this quality, other factors control his power and his strength. You will find that I have been constant in my patriotism. (322) Look at the facts. When Alexander demanded me, when they indicted me before the Amphictyonic Council, when they threatened me, when they made promises, when they set this whole damned group on me like wild animals, at no time did I betray my patriotism. From the very beginning of my political career, I chose the path of honesty and justice; I chose to foster, to increase, to associate myself with the honors, power, and reputation of our country. (323) I do not walk around the market place, with a smile on my face, exulting in the successes of our enemies, offering my hand and telling the good news to those I thought would report to Macedonia. I do not shudder and moan and hang my head when I hear of some good fortune of our city, like these impious men, who disparage our city, as if, by doing so, they are not disparaging themselves at the same time, who look abroad, who approve the

success of another—a success gained at the expense of Greece —and say that we should ensure that his success last forever.

(324) I pray to all the gods that they refuse assent to this desire but rather implant in these men a better mind and a better spirit; if they are beyond cure, may they, and they alone, be quickly and utterly destroyed, wherever they might be, and may the rest of us be granted swift release and safe security from the terrors which hang over us.

PART TWO

A
Critical
Case Study

Rhetorical Criticism:
How to Evaluate a Speech

by Jon M. Ericson

At the same time that Demosthenes was delivering speeches to the public assembly and gaining a reputation as the leading orator of his time, his contemporary, Aristotle, was privately writing that the speeches of the most successful orators could be studied, and their craftsmanship reduced to theory. Aristotle's approach to theory suggests a basic idea in the Greek's conception of art. Since any art followed a method to achieve its end, the method could be analyzed and generalizations formulated and stated as principles. In fourth-century Athens Demosthenes was the consummate artist whose methods could be observed; Aristotle was the skillful critic capable of making useful generalizations from his observations.

THE FUNCTION OF CRITICISM

The critic's task may be stated with deceptive simplicity: the critic observes public speaking in order to make useful generalizations about it.[1] The critic observes, analyzes, describes, and then evaluates. While any one of those tasks might by itself

[1] For general surveys of the principles of rhetorical criticism, see Edwin Black, *Rhetorical Criticism: A Study in Method* (New York: Macmillan,

provide justification for the critic's function, they are all never-theless subordinate to the primary purpose of formulating principles of speechmaking, or confirming principles already formulated. In short, criticism is the intellectual process which relates practice to theory and theory to practice. The critic studies speeches to add to the knowledge of speechmaking. The process is extraordinarily demanding for, ideally, the critic should begin with all of the information available to the particular speaker and add to it a full knowledge of existing rhetorical theory. The fullest possible comprehension of the speech situation is essential because the critic is, in effect, prudentially reviewing the speaker's process of preparation. A full knowledge of rhetorical theory is also necessary to confirm, revise, or enlarge what is known about speechmaking.

Before proceeding to discuss in detail the functions of the speech critic, it may be well to observe that all speech criticism is essentially evaluative. From the beginning, speech critics have used the best methods available to them to observe the speech phenomena. The methodology varies from the so-called "artistic" to that which is called "empirical," yet any method begins with a subjective evaluation about what is worth observing and ends with another evaluation regarding the usefulness of the results. Every method should be used to the extent that it contributes to our understanding of human speech.

The method and style of the orator changes with his time; so rhetorical theory is continuously adapting to the needs of a given society. Consequently, a distinction should be made between the function of the critic who is dealing with historical materials and the critic who deals with contemporary speeches. While the difference is only in emphasis, it might be said that the role of the historical critic is primarily evaluative. He evaluates the speaker's method against the established standards of that speaker's society and if the evidence warrants it he may use the results of his investigation to revise modern notions about the application of rhetorical theory in that time. The contemporary critic may do all of the foregoing and then go on to

1965); Robert Cathcart, *Post Communication: Criticism and Evaluation* (Indianapolis: Bobbs Merrill, 1966); and Lester Thonssen and A. Craig Baird, *Speech Criticism* (New York: Ronald Press, 1948).

<u>identify new methods</u> or strategies of appeal which seem to be appropriate to contemporary society. Once formulated, new principles are tested in experience and may or may not become a part of the body of accepted theory.

THE PROCESS OF CRITICISM

The actual process of criticism is much the same whether the critic's emphasis is on the evaluative or formulative function of criticism. <u>The first step in that process is the observation of the speech itself</u>. Whether or not the critic has been a member of the actual audience, he can most effectively criticize the content of the speech from an accurate manuscript of what was said. The speech itself is the object of investigation, yet the critic must devote most of his initial attention to factors external to the speech itself because it has little meaning apart from the historical circumstances which gave rise to it. Moreover, the critic must view the speech with due regard for the speaker and his audience. In short, if the critic is to make meaningful observations about the speech, he must observe the speech in relation to time, to people, and to events.

What, for example, can one say about the arguments of Demosthenes except in relation to the historical circumstances from which those arguments emerged? This speech must be viewed in the light of Aeschines' speech and in the context of Demosthenes' whole career. The relationship of the two speakers as well as each speaker's relationship to the audience must be understood. As with the speaker, so it is with the critic; there is no substitute for knowledge. The critic's task is complex because the speaker's task is complex.

The process of criticism closely parallels the process of composition, for the critic in effect is reviewing the result of the composition process. The critic views the speech as an end product—the result of a process—and describes and appraises the various rhetorical choices that combined to make up the speech. In this sense, the critic has an important concern with *results*. Accordingly, with the speech viewed as the result of a process, Demosthenes' reasoning about the relationship of the statesman to his critic would apply equally well to the orator and his critic. Demosthenes claims that his statesmanship should be judged on the basis of the choices that were made: "Consider the policy I chose in the circumstances," says Demosthenes, "don't cavil at the outcome" (192). Both Demosthenes and Aristotle employ the example of the physician to illustrate the point that, like the physician, neither the statesman nor the orator can properly be judged by the results obtained, but rather must be evaluated by the quality of the treatment. In Aristotle's words, "people who never can be well may yet be properly treated." [2] Both Demosthenes and Aristotle knew that many extraneous considerations might affect the outcome, and, accordingly, they felt the speaker must be judged by his method. Did he employ all the available means to communicate effectively? Did he construct the best possible case?

Thus, *the process of speech criticism is the observation, analysis, description, and evaluation of the speaker's employment of elements which contribute to the effective communication of his case.* While the rhetorical critic studies the speech essentially to learn about speechmaking, he is also obliged by the nature of speechmaking to involve himself in historical scholarship. Consequently, the rhetorical critic must be a capable historian and should contribute to our knowledge of history. To him, however, the reconstruction of the historical situation is a means to an end, not the primary aim of his investigation.

Once the historical context of the speech is established, the critic should clarify the central purpose of the speech. For instance, the basic purpose of the Crown speech might be stated: to determine if Demosthenes is worthy of receiving the approbation of his countrymen for his conduct of public office. The corollary assertion is obvious, but however it is stated, the critic must keep the speaker's purpose constantly before him.

In fixing the speaker's purpose, the critic should determine into what basic parts the speaker has divided the main question. These points of partition are basic because they represent vital points of contention, sometimes called "issues." Criticism then

[2] Aristotle, *The Rhetoric,* trans. by Lane Cooper (New York: Appleton-Century-Crofts, 1932), p. 7.

focuses on the speaker's ability to locate all of the relevant issues and establish them in support of his purpose. The analysis of the issues and their relevance to the speaker's purpose is often a major part of the critic's work. The Crown speech, however, exhibits no complexity with regard to the issues. There are only two issues: first, Demosthenes has, or has not, been a loyal citizen and an effective statesman; second, Aeschines has, or has not, been neither.

Observation now focuses on the means the speaker uses to accomplish his purpose. The essence of speechmaking, according to either the most ancient or the most modern theory, is that communication involves *appeal*. Traditionally, since Aristotle, the relevant appeals have included the *logical* appeal, the *pathetic* appeal, and the *ethical* appeal. In the first, the speaker appeals to the mind of his listener by attempting to cause him to identify with the speaker's process of reasoning. In effect, the speaker says, "These are the steps I took to reach this conclusion; now let me retrace those steps for you and see if you do not agree with me." The pathetic appeal identifies the speaker's purpose with the non-logical, or emotional, attitudes and beliefs of the audience. The ethical appeal identifies the speaker as a person worthy of belief. Traditional methodology has focused a great deal of attention on the speaker's inventiveness in employing these various kinds of appeals, and it has ordinarily regarded them as of prime importance. At the same time, critics have traditionally devoted attention to the appeal inherent in form itself, and have thus dealt at length with both arrangement and style (language) as means of giving effectiveness to discourse.

Demosthenes' whole speech is devoted to defense and attack utilizing all the various types of appeal. While the issues are simple enough, complex problems were imposed on the speaker. Aeschines would cloud the real issues in the legal technicalities of the indictment; moreover, he would force Demosthenes to begin his speech at his weakest point of defense and he would force Demosthenes to eulogize himself. Demosthenes minimizes these disadvantages partly by dealing with them honestly in the opening paragraphs and partly by using the "irrelevant" personal attacks of Aeschines to justify both his own sequence of material and his own personal attack on Aeschines.

While those strategies should not be overlooked as methods of appeal, they should be viewed as reactions to the setting created by Aeschines' speech and of far less consequence than Demosthenes' basic method of appeal. His basic appeal does not come from merely praising himself but from identifying himself with Athens. Thus Demosthenes appeals to the greater issue—not simply his own worth, but the worth of the Athenian democracy. He is thus able to argue on a higher plane than his rival and he is able to involve his listeners in his struggle. Demosthenes identifies himself with Athens as he states the central question of the proceedings: "What was the right policy for Athens to adopt . . . ? That is the question, men of Athens . . . and that is the issue on which I ought to be called to account. . . ." In reference to a specific act condemned by Aeschines, the speaker asks, in effect, Who did it? "Who sent reinforcements . . . who prevented the estrangement of the Hellespont . . . ? You, men of Athens; and when I say you, I mean the whole city." In another place Demosthenes puts the Athenians on trial with him as he credits them as the authors of his policies: "I am asserting these principles as your principles . . . such was the pride of Athens long before my time . . . if you condemn Ctesiphon . . . you yourselves will be adjudged as wrongdoers. . . ."

The primary strategy of Demosthenes' defense is to repeatedly identify the acts of the speaker with the highest political traditions of the audience. Moreover, the basis of his attack on Aeschines is also an appeal to the Athenian citizen's traditional concept of democratic government. The Athenian democracy moved forward with free speech—full and free deliberation, decision, and action. Demosthenes repeatedly asked his rival why he did not participate in the deliberations which led to the formulation of policy. Demosthenes appeals to the very fabric of the Greek democracy as he says that the statesman declares his judgment before the event, and accepts responsibility, while the charlatan holds his peace when he ought to speak, and then gloats over any untoward result.

After the critic has identified and described the broad bases of appeal, attention should turn to an analysis of the means used to support and reinforce those appeals. Analysis up to this point has been primarily making meaningful generalizations concerning the speaker's purpose, his determination of issues, and his basic appeals. While these generalizations are essential to subsequent analysis, criticism remains superficial unless it goes on to analyze the more particular aspects of appeal—the logical, pathetic, and ethical—appeals to reason, appeals to emotion, and appeals for the speaker on the basis of his credibility. Paradoxically, those who object most strenuously to "artistic" criticism and seek the most objective critical method are often the most reluctant to employ the scientific technique of analysis. Analysis literally means *to take apart*. While the critic may be sensitive to the fact that analysis destroys the whole, he ought not to conclude that analysis is unnecessary. Rather, the whole object can be most clearly perceived after one has closely examined the functional parts, and synthesis must follow analysis.

The critic analyzes the various arguments in support of the speaker's main contentions, with a concern for both form and substance. At this point the analytical task is often complex because the arguments are often complex and usually do not employ one method of appeal in isolation. For example, the dilemma concerning whether Aeschines rejoiced or grieved at the occasion of the Theban alliance illustrates all three methods of appeal. The critic should observe and analyze the speaker's use of language to determine his mode or modes of appeal. If he begins by looking for one type of appeal, or one type at a time, he will very likely receive a distorted view of the speech.

After analyzing the modes of appeal, the critic should give attention to the form employed by the speaker. Demosthenes uses narrative extensively and provides the critic with an excellent example of how to use expository materials to formulate effective arguments. Demosthenes varies his discourse to include analogy, specific instance, testimony, invective, contrast, and even such humor as one might find in contrasting the "stentorian tones of the orator" to the magnificent "ejaculations of the acolyte." The effective speaker usually employs a great deal of variation in the form of the discourse. In general, if the form is monotonous, the substance is not likely to be otherwise.

Closely related to the content of the speech is the arrangement of its parts. Arrangement functions as a means of persuasion because it may add to or detract from the effectiveness of the content, and because arrangement may, by itself, communicate meaning. The critic should analyze the speech to discern the principle of organization on which it is based, and he should evaluate the structure in terms of its appropriateness and effectiveness. The description of the arrangement should not be merely a summary of the content, but should instead provide perspective by representing the speech in its functional parts. The sequence of parts may, for instance, tell something about their significance. The opening paragraph of the Crown speech suggests that Demosthenes considered the sequence of his materials vital to the effectiveness of his case. In addition to inferring meaning from sequence, other inferences may be drawn from the amount of time devoted to different sections of the speech. The speaker, for example, who devotes much time to a relatively minor point may attach unintentional significance to it. Clarity gained through unity and coherence may communicate orderliness, which may in turn affect the speaker's *ethos*. In all, arrangement should be viewed as a means to an end, and the critic should evaluate it on the basis of how well it contributes to the effectiveness of the content.

Another aspect of the discourse which should be viewed as a *means* of appeal or persuasion, and not an end in itself, is the speaker's employment of language. The management of language, called *style* in a traditional description of rhetoric, has received a great deal of attention from both ancient and modern writers. While there is agreement that style deals with words or combinations of words, there was a tendency among the Greek, Roman, and Renaissance writers to deal almost exclusively with an analysis of the combinations of words—figures of speech and thought. The idea that there was a source of power—appeal or persuasiveness—in the embellishment and rhythm gained through distinctive word usage was so generally accepted that analysis followed analysis, and by the end of the Roman era more than two hundred "figures" had been identified, and Renaissance writers added to this total. Rhetoric consequently became identified with style, and style at times became identified with sophistry—the employment of style as an end in itself, or the use of language for display rather than as a means of giving effectiveness to ideas.

While classical writers gave relatively little attention to separate words, modern writers have contributed much to our comprehension of style by focusing extensively on the *meaning* of individual words. To the modern critic, words are symbols, and rhetoric functions through these symbols to make an attitude or an idea appealing. Both the modern critics I. A. Richards and Kenneth Burke recognize that whether by nature or circumstance, men are different; yet all men respond to symbols. Accordingly, criticism of style may include an investigation of language usage as a means of reducing conflict by mitigating differences. The concern is with the effectiveness, the rhetorical purpose of style—with the whole question of how words work in discourse.

In short the ancients analyzed style largely on the basis of collocations of words, while modern critics have focused on the word itself. The former method was concerned with the potential of language to appeal through distinctiveness in the form of expression. The modern method attempts to analyze the substance rather than the form as it centers on the potential appeal of the symbol itself. As in an analysis of other parts of rhetoric, the critic should consider both the form and the substance. Style in itself communicates because there is a particular power or pleasantness in a distinctive form of expression. Consequently, attention must be given to that form. Attention must also be given to the words themselves as means of giving effectiveness through a particular quality of appeal. Moreover, full attention to style also includes a consideration of the clarity and correctness of the language employed and its appropriateness to the speech. Above all, style must not be viewed as an end in itself, but as a means of appeal which serves the purpose of the speech.

In summary, the process of rhetorical criticism observes, analyzes, and describes the speech revealing the means used to express the ideas in the speech effectively. Criticism functions to evaluate and to formulate. Evaluation makes judgments about the rhetorical choices made by the speaker, and formulation follows when, on the basis of his observations, the critic adds to or revises the body of rhetorical theory.

Critical study focuses on man in an historical situation. Usually, as in the Crown speech, it focuses on man making choices in a time of crisis. From his study, the critic should not only gain new insights about the speech and about speechmaking, he should also gain a unique perspective on the man, the audience, and the issues. For these reasons critical study is humane scholarship in the most authentic sense.

A Structural Analysis of the Speech
*On the Crown**
by Francis P. Donnelly, S.J.

Demosthenes' Speech *On the Crown*

EXORDIUM

GOOD WILL FOR D. (1–8)

By request 1–2	{ D. has shown it constantly { Judges should show it fully
Through pity 3–4	{ D. may lose it; A. nothing to lose { D. has odium of self-praise; A. pleasure of abuse
By right 5–7	{ The law demands it { The defendant (second speaker) needs it. Request repeated. 8

Reprinted by permission of the publisher from *Demosthenes on the Crown*, translated by Francis P. Simpson; rhetorical commentary by Francis P. Donnelly, S.J. (New York: Fordham University Press, 1941), pp. 340–345.

° The complex relationships between the various parts of Demosthenes' speech may be seen quickly in the detailed outline provided here. The numbers used refer to sections of the speech, marked by marginal numbers in the translation. [Editor's note.]

PROPOSITION AND DIVISION (*suggested*) 9

CONFIRMATION

OUTSIDE THE INDICTMENT (10–52)

Private Life.—D. leaves it to judges (10); A.'s cunning foiled (11)

PUBLIC LIFE (12–52)

A.'s malicious method (coming years after; attacking D. through Ctes.) (12–16).

Status Translationis.

For this status, *transferring* the trial to another person, time, etc., cp. Cic. *De Inv.*, I, 16; *Ad Her.*, I. 22. The scholiasts say that, according to old commentators, D. uses this argument seventy-two times in the speech (22, 34, 83, 117, 121 sq, 139, 188, etc.).

PEACE 17–24

D. not the cause 18–20	Circumstances, the cause 18–20	Strife in Greece / Scheming of P.
	A.'s friends, the cause 21	Promoters / Abettors
D. did not prevent alliance 22–24	None proposed 22–23	No statement from A. / No embassy to Grecians
	None could be 24	It would be deceitful / It would be absurd

EMBASSY 25–52

Treachery 25–41	Ambassadors slow 25–30	D.'s law framed 25–27	To help others / To check P. in Thrace
		D.'s law ignored 28–30	A. cites a petty decree / Ambassadors loiter
	A. bribed 31–41	His deception 31–35	Furthering P.'s designs / Speaking lies
		The results 36–41	Phocis destroyed / Thebes, etc., alienated / A. shedding feigned tears
Consequences 42–52	Ruin of Greece 43–45		Thebes, etc., bewitched by P. / Other Greeks warred on by P. / D. warned a diseased country
	Ruin of traitors 46–49		General (46–47) / Particular (48–49)
	Guilt of A. 50–52		Accusing D. of A.'s crimes / Hiring himself to P. and Alex.

INSIDE THE INDICTMENT (53–296)

Proposition (53); Division (56–58); Status (59).

Justification of Ctesiphon's Decree (60–109) A.

D.'S ACTIONS FOR BEST INTERESTS OF ATHENS.

OPPOSING P. IN GENERAL 60–78

Expedient 60–65	From P.'s advantages 61–62	Greece was full of traitors / Greece was divided
	From D.'s policy 63–65	Alternatives were alliance or neutrality / Athens fared better than allies or neutrals
Honorable 66–68	From policy 66–67	Of Athens / Of P.
	From antecedents 68	Of P. / Of Athens
Just 69–78	From aggressions of P. 69–72	Remote / Recent
	From documentary proofs 73–78	Decrees acquit D. of starting war / Letter of P. absolves D.

OPPOSING P. IN PARTICULAR 79–109

Abroad 79–101	Expeditions 79–94	Summary described (79); proved best (80) / Euboea described (81–82); proved best (83–86) / Byzantium described (87–88); proved best (89–94)
	Disinterested policy 95–101	Against Sparta for Thebes and Corinth / Against Thebes for Sparta / Against Thebes for Euboea / In many precedents for D.'s actions
At home 102–109	Enactment of naval law 102–106	Against injustices / Despite prosecutions / Despite attempted bribery
	Excellence of naval law 107–109	Successful in war / Best for interests of city / Identical in spirit with D.'s policy abroad

Conclusion and transition, 110.

Legality of Ctesiphon's Decree (111–125)

A's CHARGES 111–121

Accountability
111–119
{ Law demands account for office only (111–112)
Ctes. praised D. for gifts (113)
Precedents justify Ctes.' act (114–117)
A. indicts thanks for gifts; not fact of gifts (118–119)

Proclamation
120–121
{ Proclamation often had
Proclamation for good of people
Proclamation prescribed at times by law

A's SPIRIT 121–125

Spiteful
121–122
{ Garbling laws
Arbitrarily defining a statesman

Perverse
123
{ Accusation deals with laws; abuse with calumny
Courts are for convictions; not for contumely

Hostile to city
124–125
{ Avoiding a possible conviction
Urging an impossible conviction

Justification of Ctesiphon's Decree
(126–296) B.

INDIRECT DEFENSE (126–159)
D'S OPPOSITION TO A., PHILIP'S FRIEND

PRIVATE LIFE OF A. 126–131

Character
126–128
{ Worthless
Hypocritical

Parents
129–131
{ Disgraceful in their beginning
Absurd in their pretensions
Unfortunate in their son

PUBLIC LIFE OF A. 132–159

Before war, P.'s ally
132–138
{ Antiphon
Python
Anaxinus

Afterwards, P.'s tool in Amphissian War 139–159

- A.'s guilt 139–140
  - Enacts no laws to check P.
  - Strives volubly to escape Amphissian charge
- D.'s opposition 141–144
  - Solemnly protests truth now
  - Vainly protested formerly
- Plans of P. 145–148
  - Without Thebes, etc., P. could not reach Athens
  - Without Amph. Council, P. could not persuade Thebes
  - Without an Athenian, P. could not deceive Amph. Council
- Co-operation of A. 149–151
  - A. elected delegate
  - A. proposes an attack on Amphissia
  - Amphictyonic Council calls in P.
- Results 152–159
  - P. captures Elatea
  - D. checks P. by Theban Alliance
  - A. is cause of Greeks' downfall

DIRECT DEFENSE—Positively

D.'S ACTIONS FOR BEST INTERESTS OF ATHENS
(160–251)

THEBAN ALLIANCE 160–226

Beginning 160–210

- Enmity of Thebes 160–168
  - Opposed by D.
  - Opposed by Arist. and Eubu.
  - Fostered by A. and P.
- News of Elatea 169–188
  - Tumult
  - D.'s measures (174–188)
- Value of D.'s measures 188–210
  - Only possible course then or now 188–191
  - Only prudent course; best for Athens; better than A.'s course 192–198
  - Only honorable course; following precedent, without mistake 199–210

Completion 211–226

- The acts 211–226
  - Persuasion of Thebes 211–214
  - Campaign 215–216
- Their appraisal 217–226
  - By Aeschines (217)
  - By Philip (218)
  - By Demosthenes (219–221)
  - By decree (222–226)

ALL D.'s ACTS 227–251

Before Chæronea 227–243	A.'s reckoning 227–231	Condemns himself (228)
		Omits opposite evils (229–230)
		Omits positive benefit (231)
	D.'s reckoning 232–243	Situation of Athens, P., D. 234–236
		Measures of D. 237–243
Chæronea 244–247	Not due to D. as ambassador 244	D. victorious
		P. uses force
	Not due to D. as statesman 245–246	Not master of life and fortune
		Successful in statesman's work
	Due to arms and bribery 247	D. not leader of army
		D. not bribed by P.
After Chæronea 248–251	D. elected 248	To safeguard city
		To be food commissioner
	D. acquitted 249–251	In various trials
		Never indicted by A.

DIRECT DEFENSE—Negatively (*Refutation*)

D. NOT TO BLAME FOR ATHENS' WOES (252–296)

FORTUNE 252–275

Of Athens 252–255	Good	
	Better than that of other cities	
	Not controlled by D.'s fortune	
Of opponents 256–269	Demosthenes— 256–257	Private
		Public
	Aeschines—258–264	Private
		Public
	Both—265–269	Comparison
		Proof
Of Athens 270–275	Not due to D.	All people have suffered
		D. not the only statesman
	D. unjustly accused by A.	A. did not come forward before
		A. blames even the accidental

ELOQUENCE 276–296

Eloquence of A. hostile 276–284	To individuals 276–281	{ Attacking from spite { Attacking to show off eloquence
	To State 281–284	{ Fraternizing with P. { Pretending to be P.'s friend
Eloquence of D. patriotic 285–290	D. gave funeral oration 285–287	{ A. and party were enemies { Exulted with P. over Chæronea
	D. had funeral meal at house 288–290	{ Nearest to all bereaved { Justified by public inscription
Eloquence of A. traitorous 291–296	Exulting over Chæronea 291–293	{ Not sad over Athens' defeat { Attacked Athenian principles
	Responsible for ruin of Athens 293–296	{ Same acts as other traitors { Same principles as other traitors

Peroration (297–324)

D. is worthy 297–306	No traitor 297–298	{ Resisted all temptations { True as beam of balance
	True patriot 299–302	{ Building material wall { Building national wall
	Successful statesman 303–306	{ Left nothing undone { All would be free, if D. had assistants
A. is unworthy 307–313	Traitor 307–308	{ Assisting enemy { Keeping treacherous silence
	Unsuccessful statesman 309–313	{ Measures (309–311) { Money contributions (312–313)
D. and the ancients 314–324	Comparison with ancients unfair 314–317	{ They are respected; living are envied { Their great benefits do not destroy our smaller ones { They are akin to D. not to A.
	Comparison with contemporaries fair 318–324	{ As in all contests { With A.'s party traitors, before and now

PROPOSITION (*entire speech*): Ctes.' decree is lawful.

PROPOSITION (*omitting* 111–121 *and digressions, e.g., private life*): D. acted for the best interests of Athens.

STATUS: Because D. opposed P. (A. is shown to be P.'s friend and was opposed by D.)

SYLLOGISM: He who opposed P. acted for the best interests of Athens. But D. opposed P.

The general question of opposing P. and safeguarding Athenian liberty is discussed principally in 60–72, 95–102, 188–210, by an appeal to precedents. The particular measures of D. are proved in each case advantageous by a presentation of the facts, corroborated by documents.

POINTS IN DISPUTE: I The grounds or justification of Ctes.' decree; II The omitted proviso, "When he has handed in his accounts." (Accountability): III The proclamation in the theater.

ORDER: In Ctes.' decree and A.'s indictment. I, II, III: in A.'s speech, II, III, I; in D.'s speech I (outside indictment, 10–52; inside indictment, A, 53–110), II, III, I (inside indictment, B; indirect defense, 126-159; direct defense, 160–296).

Demosthenes' Use of History

by Charles Rann Kennedy

This has justly been considered the greatest speech of the greatest orator in the world. It derives an additional interest from the circumstance that it was the last great speech delivered in Athens. The subject matter of it is virtually a justification of the whole public policy and life of Demosthenes; while in point of form it is a defense of Ctesiphon for a decree which he proposed in favor of Demosthenes, B.C. 338, not long after the battle of Chæronea.

When the news of that disastrous battle reached Athens, the people were in the utmost consternation. Nothing less was expected than an immediate invasion of Attica by the conqueror; and strong measures were taken, under the advice of Hyperides, to put the city in a posture of defense. One of the most important was the repair of the walls and ramparts. Demosthenes at this time held the office of conservator of walls, having been appointed by his own tribe at the end of the year B.C. 339. The reparation, which had been commenced before, but sus-

Reprinted from *The Orations of Demosthenes On the Crown and On The Embassy,* translated, with notes, by Charles Rann Kennedy (London: George Bell and Sons, 1884; Bohn's Classical Library), pp. 1–9.

pended during the late campaign, was now vigorously prosecuted. He himself superintended the work, and expended on it
three talents of his own money, beyond what was allowed out
of the public treasury.

The fears of the people were not realized. Philip, while he
chastised the Thebans, treated the Athenians with moderation
and clemency; restoring their prisoners without ransom, bury-
ing their dead upon the field, and sending their bones to Athens.
He deprived them indeed of most of their foreign possessions,
but even enlarged their domestic territory by the addition of
Oropus.

It seemed that the whole foundation upon which the credit
and influence of Demosthenes had rested was overthrown. The
hopes which he had held out of successful resistance to Philip,
of re-establishing Athenian ascendancy, or maintaining the independence of Greece, were now proved to be fallacious. The
alliance of Thebes, his last great measure for the protection of
Athens, appeared to have been the immediate cause of her defeat and disgrace. The very moderation with which Philip had
used his victory looked like a reproach to the orator, who had
so often denounced his cruelties before the Athenian assembly,
and warned them of his deadly hostility to Athens.

The Macedonian party considered that the time has come
for the humiliation of their adversary. They assailed him with
prosecutions. The peace which Athens concluded with Macedonia was the signal for war against Demosthenes. But his enemies were mistaken in their reckoning, when they supposed
that the people would feel resentment against him as the author of their misfortunes. The Athenians took a juster and no-
bler view of the matter: they judged not of his counsels by the
result, but by their own intrinsic merit. Demosthenes came
clear and triumphant out of every prosecution; and while Lysi-
cles the general was condemned to capital punishment for his
misconduct of the war, Demosthenes received from his countrymen a signal proof of their esteem and confidence, being
appointed to pronounce the funeral oration in honor of the citizens who had fallen at Chæronea.

About the same time, and not many months after the battle,
Ctesiphon introduced a bill to the Council of Five Hundred,

proposing to reward Demosthenes for his gifts of money to the public, and for his general integrity and good conduct as a statesman. It is not unlikely that the very object of this measure was to stop the attacks upon Demosthenes, and to give him the opportunity, in case it should be opposed, of justifying the whole course of his political life. With that view was inserted the clause eulogizing his general character as a statesman. The Macedonian party naturally regarded this clause as a reflection upon themselves, and a virtual condemnation of the policy which they had for so many years espoused. They felt themselves therefore compelled to make a stand against it; and they resolved upon a course, which was open to them according to the Athenian laws, of indicting Ctesiphon as the author of an illegal measure. His bill, having been approved by the council, and then brought before the popular assembly, was passed in the shape of a decree, by which it was declared to be the will of the council and people of Athens, "that Demosthenes should be presented with a golden crown, and that a proclamation should be made in the theater, at the great Dionysian festival, at the performance of the new tragedies, announcing that Demosthenes was rewarded by the people with a golden crown for his integrity, for the goodwill which he had invariably displayed towards all the Greeks and towards the people of Athens, and also for his magnanimity, and because he had ever both by word and deed promoted the interests of the people, and been zealous to do all the good in his power." This decree, as the opposite party conceived, was open to three objections, two of which were chiefly of a legal nature; the other, while it equally assumed a legal form, called in question the real merits of Ctesiphon's motion. An indictment, embodying all the objections, was preferred before the archon, the chief magistrate of Athens, to whose cognizance a criminal proceeding of this kind appertained. The prosecutor was Aeschines, the second of Athenian orators, the deadly enemy of Demosthenes, who would not only be considered by his party as the fittest person to conduct the cause, but was stimulated to it by every motive of rivalry and revenge. The indictment, after reciting the decree, alleged that it violated the Athenian laws in three points, as follows:—

First, because it was unlawful to make false allegations in any of the state documents:

Secondly, because it was unlawful to confer a crown upon any person who had an account to render of his official conduct; and Demosthenes was both a conservator of walls and a treasurer of the theoric fund:

Thirdly, because it was unlawful to proclaim the honor of a crown in the theater at the Dionysian festival, at the performance of the new tragedies; the law being, that if the council gave a crown, it should be published in the council-hall; if the people, in the pnyx at the popular assembly.

The first of these points raised the substantial question at issue—viz., whether the decree of Ctesiphon had stated a falsehood, when it assigned the virtue and patriotism of Demosthenes as reasons for conferring public honor upon him. The other two, while they were mainly of a technical character, were strongly relied on by Aeschines as affording him the means of securing a verdict.

Notice of intention to indict had probably been given at the time when the decree was passed. The bill was actually preferred on the sixth of Elaphebolion, B.C. 338, eight months after the battle of Chæronea, and a few days before the Dionysian festival, at which the honor conferred upon Demosthenes was to have been proclaimed. It had this immediate consequence, that the decree of Ctesiphon could not be carried into effect till after the trial; and thus one end, at least, was gained by Aeschines and his party—the satisfaction of having suspended their adversary's triumph. But whether they were deterred by the failure of other prosecutions against Demosthenes, or whether they judged from the temper of the people that they had but little chance of success, the indictment of Ctesiphon was suffered to lie dormant for more than seven years, and was not brought to trial till the year B.C. 330. It may seem strange that the law of Athens should have allowed a criminal prosecution to hang over a man for so long a period; but it must be borne in mind that the proceeding against Ctesiphon not only involved a charge personally affecting him, but had the further, and ostensibly the more important, object of maintaining the purity of the law itself, and preventing an unconstitutional decree from being recorded in the public archives. It is probable, however, that the case would never have been revived, but for the occurrence of political events which seemed to afford a favorable opportunity.

Within two years after his victory at Chæronea, Philip had perished by the hand of an assassin. The hopes that were excited in Greece by the news of his death were quickly dispelled by the vigorous measures of his successor. Notwithstanding the efforts of Demosthenes, it was found impossible to concert any feasible plan for a union of the Greek states against Macedonia. The rash revolt of the Thebans was punished by the extirpation of their city, which struck terror into the very heart of Greece. Athens, suspected of aiding the insurgents, hastened to appease the conqueror by humble submission; and when he insisted on the delivery up of their principal orators, including Demosthenes, it was with difficulty that he was prevailed upon to accept a less severe measure of satisfaction. The debate which took place in the Athenian assembly upon this demand of Alexander shows that Demosthenes must still have been in high esteem at Athens. The feelings of the people, notwithstanding their fears, were against the delivery of the orators; and Phocion's counsel, urging them to surrender themselves for the public good, was not well received. Alexander in the year following (B.C. 334) passed over into Asia, and commenced his career of conquest. Meanwhile Greece had a breathing time. The states that sighed for freedom looked with anxious expectation for every intelligence from the scene of war, as if all their hopes depended on the fate of one man. The further he penetrated into Asia, the better chance there seemed to be of his being overwhelmed by the force of the Persian empire. While he was yet in the defiles of Cilicia, it was confidently asserted by Demosthenes at Athens, that his army would be trampled under foot by the cavalry of Darius. The battle of Issus belied this prophecy; yet it was still believed that the Persian monarchy had resources in itself sufficient to prevail in the war: and the length of time that Alexander was occupied in Phœnicia and Egypt, whilst Darius was collecting the strength of his empire in the East, seemed to favor these sanguine views.

About the time that Alexander was marching to fight his

last and decisive battle against the Persian king in Mesopotamia, Agis, king of Sparta, put himself at the head of a confederacy, which comprised the greater part of the Peloponnesian states, and prepared to throw off the Macedonian yoke. Taking his opportunity, whilst Antipater was engaged in suppressing a Thracian insurrection, he raised his standard in Laconia, and declared war; but, after gaining some successes and laying siege to Megalopolis, which refused to join the league, he was defeated in a hard-fought battle by Antipater, and died fighting with the valor of an ancient Spartan. This was in the beginning of the year B.C. 330. The confederacy was dissolved, and the voice of freedom was again changed to that of submission.

Athens had taken no part in the last movement. The cause of her neutrality is not quite clear, though it is probably to be attributed to a want of proper concert and preparation. Had the Athenians sent their forces to assist Agis in Peloponnesus, they would have been exposed to the first attack of the enemy, and the dread of this may have restrained them from rising. A Macedonian garrison was maintained in the Cadmea, which would gain speedy intelligence of any movement on the part of the Athenians, and the people of the Bœotian towns were friendly to Macedonia. It is not quite clear either what part Demosthenes took upon this occasion. Aeschines represents him as boasting that he had kindled the flames of war in Peloponnesus; and both Plutarch and Dinarchus intimate that he exerted himself for that purpose: yet Aeschines accuses him also of neglecting so good an opportunity for engaging Athens in the contest. Demosthenes may in prudence have abstained from plunging the Athenians into a war, for which he saw they were ill prepared, and at the same time he may have encouraged the Peloponnesians to make an effort of which, in the event of success, his own country would equally have reaped the benefit. So timid a policy he would not certainly have adopted eight years before; but under existing circumstances it could hardly be a reproach to him, especially when he observed the timid and temporizing spirit which was gradually gaining ground among his countrymen. Presents of Persian spoil had been sent to Athens, to decorate the Acropolis. Phocion corresponded with Alexander as a friend; and it was generally represented by all who belonged to his party, that resistance to him was hopeless.

If such feelings prevailed to a great extent before the defeat of Agis, they must have been greatly strengthened after that event. Macedonian arms were everywhere triumphant. Alexander had seated himself on the throne of Darius; Antipater, his viceroy, was irresistible in Greece: Macedonian ascendancy, which Demosthenes had exerted himself all his life to oppose, seemed now to be completely secured. Athens was not what she was even at the time of Chæronea. For sixteen years before that disastrous battle, the voice of Demosthenes had been continually resounding in the assembly, instructing, animating, improving, elevating the minds and hearts of his hearers; exerting such an influence over them, that he may be said to have raised up, by the force of his own eloquence, a new generation of patriots. But in the eight years that followed it was very different. His voice in the cause of freedom and glory had been little heard; and besides that the people were cowed by the events which had occurred, a lethargy had fallen on their spirit, for want of someone to rouse them.

This was the time chosen by Aeschines for bringing to an issue the long-suspended cause. The aspect of affairs both at home and abroad seemed favorable to the undertaking; and he summoned up all his force and resolution for the contest. It was to be not only a trial of strength between the contending parties at Athens,—the favorers of Macedonian power, and those that regretted the loss of independence,—but a final and decisive struggle between two rival statesmen, exasperated against each other by a long series of hostilities. It was manifest that Ctesiphon was but the nominal defendant; the real object of attack was Demosthenes, his whole policy and administration. The interest excited was intense, not only at Athens, but throughout all Greece; and an immense concourse of foreigners flocked from all parts to hear the two most celebrated orators in the world. A jury (of not less than 500) was impanelled by the archon; and before a dense and breathless audience the pleadings began.

As the speeches of both the orators are preserved to us, we have the means of comparing one with the other, and forming our opinion of their respective merits. The world in general have decided as the people of Athens did, not only upon the oratorical merits of the two rivals, but upon the principal questions at issue between them. The accuser, who thought to brand his opponent with eternal infamy, has only added to the luster of his renown. Independently of the internal evidence furnished by this and other orations of Demosthenes, which have carried to the hearts of most readers a conviction of his patriotism, we cannot fail to be strongly influenced by the judgment of the Athenians themselves, whom neither their own past misfortunes, nor the terror inspired by the late victory of Antipater, could deter from giving a verdict, by which, while they acquitted Demosthenes from all blame, they in effect declared their approbation of his measures in opposition to Macedonia.

The reader who carefully examines the speech of Aeschines will not fail to observe, that he betrays a consciousness of weakness in that part of his case where he attacks the political character of his rival. He seems to feel also that he is speaking in opposition to the general feeling of his hearers. His own character as a politician had been so dubious, his conduct so open to suspicion, that while he most bitterly assails his adversary, he is constantly under the necessity of defending himself. On the whole life, public and private, of Demosthenes, he pours a torrent of invective; to this the greater part of his speech is devoted: yet he seems to have been impelled to it rather by hate and revenge, than by any calculation of advantage. On the other hand, when he deals with the legal parts of his case, commenting on those specific violations of Athenian law which Ctesiphon's measure was charged with, it is evident that his strength lay there; he handles his subject temperately, skillfully, and carefully, laboring to make every point clear to the jury, and to impress them with the conviction that to uphold the laws was the sure way to maintain constitutional government. On these points he mainly relied, hoping by this means to secure a verdict, which would give him a triumph over his enemy, and carry the general opinion over Greece, that the credit and influence of Demosthenes were extinguished.

Demosthenes, feeling his weakness as to the legal questions, dexterously throws them into the middle of his speech, and passes lightly and rapidly over them, while he devotes his greatest efforts to the vindication of his own merits as a patriot and a statesman. Refusing to comply with the insidious demand of Aeschines, that he should take the questions in the same order as his accuser, he insists upon his legal right to conduct his defense as he pleases. Opening with a modest exordium, to conciliate the favor of the jury, he launches gradually into the history of his own conduct and measures: presenting first a general view of the condition of Greece when he entered public life, and of the difficulties under which the Athenians labored in their contest with Philip; then setting forth his own views, plans, and objects, and showing that he had advised a course of action which both the circumstances of the time and the honor of the country required. He apologizes for the self-praise mixed up with his speech, on the ground that he was driven to it by his opponent. Entering on the Sacred War, and the peace of B.C. 346, he labors to exculpate himself from all share in errors then committed, imputing them chiefly to the negligence of the other ambassadors, and to the treachery of Philocrates and Aeschines, who, by the false hopes which they excited at Athens, prevented the people from assisting the Phocians. Coming to the events which brought on a renewal of the war, he shows how Philip's ambitious projects and encroachments in every part of Greece made it necessary to oppose him, especially for the Athenians, who were menaced at home as well as abroad by his aggression in Thrace, Eubœa, and Megara. He pursues these topics until he has carried with him the feelings of his hearers, which must have been strongly on his side when he dilated on the glorious issue of the campaigns in Eubœa and the Propontis, and read to them the decrees of the Byzantines, Perinthians, and Chersonesites, in honor of Athens, all which were due to the vigorous measures of his own administration. Having thus secured the goodwill and sympathy of his judges, he proceeds to discuss the legal charges against Ctesiphon. Dwelling on them but for a short time, he plunges into a personal attack upon Aeschines, holding up to ridicule the meanness of his birth and parentage, and retorting on him the same coarse and opprobrious language which had been used towards himself. The bitterness of his invective is only to be excused on the ground of strong provocation, added to an assurance that his more grave charges of corruption and treason were well founded. Those charges, so often advanced before, he here repeats, denouncing more particularly the conduct of Aeschines upon his mission to Delphi, B.C. 339, to which the disaster of Chæronea was attributable. The account which Aeschines had given of this affair he shows to be false, and enters upon a minute examination of the proceedings which caused Philip to be appointed Amphictyonic general, and to march with an invading army, nominally against the Amphissian Locrians, really against Bœotia and Attica. A graphic description is given of the consternation at Athens on hearing that Philip had seized Elatea. The meeting of the people, the advice of Demosthenes to them, his embassy to Thebes, the success of his negotiations, and the conclusion of the alliance between Thebes and Athens are briefly recounted, Demosthenes forcibly pointing out the advantage of his measures, contending that they were not to be judged by the mere event of the battle, and that it was far more glorious for his country to be defeated in a struggle for the independence of Greece, than it would have been to keep aloof from the contest. Here he makes that noble adjuration, which has in all ages been admired, appealing to his countrymen by the deeds of their ancestors, of whom they would have acted most unworthily, had they without a struggle abandoned the post of honor bequeathed to them. He himself as a statesman would have deserved execration, had he advised such a course. The failure of their arms was not to be imputed to the minister, who had done all he could to insure their success, but rather to the commanders, or to evil fortune. As Aeschines had said so much about the ill fortune which attended him, he draws a comparison between the different fortunes of himself and his rival, first, of their early life and education, next, of their career as public men. Aeschines from the beginning had taken a part which put him in opposition to the true interests of Athens, which caused him to rejoice at her disasters, to quail and tremble at her successes. He never came forward to assist her by his counsels when she needed them, but only to censure others who had given their honest advice, because it had not turned out as well as was expected. It was a signal proof of his malignant disposition, that he had expatiated on the late disastrous events as if they were a subject of triumph to him, without shedding a single tear, without any faltering in his voice, without betraying the least emotion or symptom of grief. In reply to the challenge of Aeschines, to say for what merit he claimed the reward of a crown, Demosthenes boldly declares, for his incorruptibility, by which he was distinguished not only from Aeschines, but from the multitude of venal orators in the Grecian world. Had there been but a few more like himself in other states, Macedonia could never have risen to greatness upon their ruins. He had done all that was possible for a single man; and Athens, while she shared the misfortune of all the Greeks, had the consolation of reflecting, that she had striven gallantly and bravely to avert the common calamity. Aeschines had lauded the great men of a bygone age, drawing an invidious contrast between Demosthenes and them. This, says Demosthenes, was not a fair way of judging him: he should be tried by reference to his own acts, as compared with those of his contemporaries. Yet even from the former comparison he did not shrink; for he had acted on the same principles as the statesmen of olden time, striving always to maintain the honor and dignity of Athens. Attachment to his country, and earnest anxiety for her welfare, had been his constant and abiding motives of action: throughout his whole life, in the day of power, in the hour of trial and adversity, those feelings had never deserted him: that was the test of a good and honest citizen; by that he ought to be judged.

Such is, in substance, the argument of this celebrated oration, as far as relates to the main question in the cause. The effect produced by the speech upon an Athenian audience can be but faintly imagined by us who read it at this distance of time. Although Athens was not then what she had once been; although she was humbled by defeat, shorn of her honors, stripped of her empire and dependencies, without allies, without resources, without means of resistance to that iron power under which all Greece had succumbed; there was still the remembrance of the past, not yet extinguished by habitual servitude; there were still vague hopes of future deliverance, and a fire of smothered indignation burning in the hearts of the people, ready to burst into a flame at the first favorable opportunity. That such were their feelings is proved by what occurred seven years afterwards upon the death of Alexander; when Athens made one convulsive effort for freedom, ere she finally submitted to her fate. Demosthenes stood before his countrymen, representing all which remained of Athenian dignity and glory. If any man could help them, it was he. His advice had always been steady and constant; his warnings should have been earlier attended to: but even yet there might be need of him. He was their consolation for the past, their hope for the future. During the progress of his address, such thoughts rushed upon their minds with greater and greater force, till they were elevated above themselves, and all the spirit of their ancestors was for the moment regenerated within them.

They could forgive him all his egotism and self-praise. It was the praise of a life devoted to their service. Where he lauded his own acts most strongly, he identified them with the glories of his country. Whatever good results might have accrued from his measures, he ascribed the merit less to himself than to the fortune of Athens, or to the gods, of whom he was but the humble instrument in a righteous cause. His own eloquence would have been of no avail, had it not touched the true chord of Athenian feeling. Throughout his whole political career he had been supported by the judgment and convictions of the people. Thus he argued, and the people felt it was impossible for them to find him guilty, without passing sentence upon themselves, without condemning the policy which Athens had for a long series of years consistently pursued. The genius of Athens protected her from such disgrace; and by an overwhelming majority, which left the accuser no choice but to retire into exile, a verdict was given for the defendant.

Demosthenes' Use of Argument

by Donovan J. Ochs

A great many modern readers seem to feel that it is not worth their while to read a speech by someone as ancient as Demosthenes. This is a mistake, for a great deal can be learned from observing a master craftsman like Demosthenes. His artistry, even though shaped by the circumstances of his own time, has a "time-less" quality that can be appreciated readily by a modern reader who is willing to look objectively at the speech *On the Crown.*

Assessed merely from the standards of modern rhetorical taste Demosthenes' speech *On the Crown* may seem to fall short on many counts. Many students of speech criticism are quick to censure the speech for its excessive length and for its numerous historical references and allusions, which seem removed from their present interest and understanding. The speech can also be reproached on the grounds that the issues no longer seem relevant. It is insufficient rebuttal to these charges to contend that a speech must be judged within its full historic and cultural context, for such an appraisal, in this instance, presupposes an exhaustive study of fifth- and fourth-century history, politics, economics, sociology, education, etc. Furthermore, to argue that the true greatness of Demosthenes' defense can only be appreciated by reading the speech in the original Greek, in effect removes the problem by removing the speech from English-speaking students.

If, moreover, one must re-create in complete detail the life and times of Demosthenes to understand and fully appreciate the Crown speech, then perhaps the sheer effort far outweighs any advantage in undertaking a study of Demosthenes' defense of Ctesiphon. One cannot understand the art of a speaker's choice and deployment of arguments apart from the socio-political milieu which create the necessity for a particular speech. Some degree of involvement with the historic context is necessary, of course, to cope with Demosthenes' strategy of defense.

If any artifact is to be credited with the encomium of a "classic," then something must be contained within the artifact itself which is either useful or enjoyable or valuable for some reason—but useful, enjoyable, or valuable to each succeeding generation.

Therefore this essay rests on the principle that studying the use by a master craftsman of the tools of argumentation is, at one and the same time, an invitation to gain fruitful insights into the theory of argumentation and, on an aesthetic level, an opportunity to enjoy the graceful artistry of a professional orator-statesman at the zenith of his oratorical career.

Precisely what did Demosthenes confront as he began his defense? We know that he addressed a jury composed of several hundred Athenian citizens. As Athenians they had undoubtedly heard Demosthenes many times before; consequently, his reputation as an orator was already established. As Athenians, however, we can be certain that many of the jurors had either personally fought at Chæronea or had lost relatives in the battle with Alexander. Demosthenes, therefore, could expect little sympathy from men whom he had assured of success and exhorted to war only to suffer the ignominy of defeat. It is a truism of politics that when any nation loses a war, scapegoats become necessary. Demosthenes had advocated war, the war was lost, therefore his countrymen could conclude that Demosthenes' policy had caused the Athenian defeat.

Moreover, the jury had spent most of the morning listening

to Aeschines' prosecution. Consequently, Demosthenes had to overcome not only the failure of his policy and the resistance of an unsympathetic audience but the arguments of Aeschines as well.

AESCHINES' INTRODUCTION

If we turn again for a moment to the issues raised by the prosecution we find that Aeschines used a number of cultural appeals around which he structured the proem for his case. For example, Aeschines implied in his remarks on "the attempts to halt the actual trial" that those who are fearful of justice are probably guilty of injustice. More than a mere appeal to the juror's benevolence was contained in the prosecution's "reliance on the gods, the laws, and the judges." Aeschines had subtly suggested that Demosthenes and his followers had set themselves against the gods and the law; consequently, Demosthenes should be presumed guilty from the outset of the trial. The theme of Demosthenes' impiety received more attention in Aeschines' diatribe on Demosthenes' character. Not without purpose did Aeschines discuss "the old legal procedures which restrained public speakers." This discussion served as a circuitous attack on Demosthenes' customary mode of delivery by means of anticipatory refutation. Aeschines assumed that Demosthenes would counter his prosecution with a highly polished, *emotional* defense. If Demosthenes did become "unrestrained" then the jury could remember that Aeschines forecast such a method of defense. Further, Aeschines suggested that lack of restraint by orators had partially been the cause for the liberal revision of Solon's systems of legal and deliberative procedure. Demosthenes, therefore, confronted a rhetorical dilemma. If he began with restraint, he risked losing the case by virtue of apparent indifference. If he was unrestrained, Demosthenes faced the juror's predisposition that he was, by virtue of his lack of restraint, responsible for tampering with the revered legal and deliberative systems.

Aeschines applied one further premise to the foundation of his introductory attack. Without mentioning either Demosthenes or Ctesiphon—to do so was totally unnecessary—Aeschines moved to a philosophical digression on "the role of established law in a democracy." By equating "prosecution for violation of laws" with "upholding democracy," Aeschines accomplished a four-fold end. First, he had posited a generally agreed upon principle of political behavior from which he could move into the several points of the indictment. Second, since the jury realized he was about to demonstrate that Demosthenes did violate the law, he emplanted the consequence of acquitting any person who broke the law, namely, the dissolution and erosion of the Athenian political ideal, democracy. Third, since Aeschines knew that the laws in this instance clearly favored the prosecution, he placed Demosthenes in the unenviable position of arguing for his innocence as well as justifying the loss of Athenian democracy. Fourth, by not referring specifically to Demosthenes, Aeschines appeared to be speaking from the vantage point of one who espoused equity, democracy, and a conservative return to justice under the law—vantage points far above the actual indictment.

ARGUMENTS OF THE INDICTMENT ADVANCED BY AESCHINES

A close reading of the abstract of Aeschines' speech found in this volume will reveal three primary charges of illegality against Ctesiphon: (1) that Ctesiphon proposed the Crown at a time when Demosthenes had not been audited; (2) that Ctesiphon's decree specified that the honorific Crown be presented to Demosthenes in the theatre; and (3) that falsehoods, namely, Demosthenes' life of public service for the benefit of Greece, were inserted into Ctesiphon's decree.

Although these three arguments served as the primary structure of Aeschines' prosecution, numerous related issues were raised. For example, under the first charge of illegality, Aeschines not only established the existence of a law expressly forbidding anyone to propose a Crown for an unaudited magistrate, but he also resorted to anticipatory refutation. If Demosthenes should attempt to answer the obvious illegality by contending that he was an "inspector," not a "magistrate," then Demosthenes is guilty because another law equated inspectors and magistrates. If Demosthenes should argue that he used his

own funds, the law, as entered on record by Aeschines, finds
Demosthenes guilty. If Demosthenes should argue that he was,
in fact, not accountable when Ctesiphon proposed the decree,
then Demosthenes must somehow demonstrate that the Senate
calendar, as entered on record by Aeschines, was in error. If
Demosthenes should elect to base his defense on the grounds
that, since he was neither appointed by lot nor chosen by the
people, he was not legally a magistrate, then Demosthenes
would have to argue against the law which held persons appointed by their tribes as magistrates. Aeschines, therefore, not
only establishes the illegality of the first charge, but effectively
reduces possible stances for the defense.

The same tactic of removing the argumentative basis from
his opposition characterizes Aeschines' relatively perfunctory
treatment of the second charge, i.e., the illegality of proclaiming the Crown in the theatre. The letter of the law was not only
read to the jury, but the spirit of the law was explained by
Aeschines. Quite simply the law stated that if the Senate
crowned a person, the proclamation had to occur in the Senate,
if the people, in the Assembly.

Aeschines imputed motives of self-aggrandizement to Demosthenes by his gloss on the law concerning proclamations. In
essence he said that one honored by the Athenians should not
be pompously displayed to foreigners. Anticipating Demosthenes' introduction of a contradictory law in this defense, Aeschines first demonstrated that contradictory laws are impossible.
Elected magistrates checked all laws annually and eliminated
those that were contradictory. Aeschines then discussed the
two laws concerning proclamations of Crowns. One law governed those persons crowned by the people in which case the
proclamation had to occur in the Assembly. A second law
governed those crowned by their own tribes (Ctesiphon and
Demosthenes belonged to the same tribe) without a decree, in
which case the proclamation could not take place in the theatre.

Had Aeschines halted his attack after presenting the legal
issues the verdict might well have been reversed. Demosthenes'
diversionary strategy would have been blatantly apparent and,
as a result, Demosthenes would be essentially restricted to a

defense of the legality of Ctesiphon's proposal. From the fact that Aeschines chose to continue his harangue by means of an *ad hominem* attack on the life, character, and policy of his opponent we can safely conjecture that, indeed, the legal issues were of little consequence to Aeschines. Only his hatred for Demosthenes and a near psychotic desire for revenge could have motivated his subsequent assault.

A marked shift in tone and argumentative techniques occurred as Aeschines moved into his wholesale attack on Demosthenes under the guise of the illegality of inserting falsehoods into decrees. Allusions were made to Demosthenes as a base-born, petty, treacherous, dishonest, intemperate, and inconsistent individual in his personal affairs. Demosthenes was variously accused, primarily by vitriolic assertion, of betraying Thrace to Philip, of pandering to the Macedonian ambassadors, of accepting bribes from the enemies of Athens, of impiety since he supported the Locrians, a tribe who cultivated cursed soil, of sending the Thebans to certain death, and of abandoning his position at Chæronea.

After Aeschines had completed his attack on Demosthenes' life, character, and policy, he interjected a series of commonplaces. Although these stock arguments were frequently employed by fourth-century orators, these expanded themes probably carried some amount of argumentative weight. Excessive awards, said Aeschines, render the giving of awards meaningless. Comparisons and contrasts were made between the old Athenian custom of granting honors to only a few worthy persons and the more recent practice of making frequent awards to undeserving individuals. The standard theme elaborated on is that anyone who assists a defendant to propose illegal measures destroys the constitution. Since Demosthenes had received a Crown from the Athenians prior to the indictment, Aeschines seems to imply that even if Ctesiphon is found innocent, Demosthenes ought not receive the Crown. Other commonplaces suggested that if Ctesiphon were to be found innocent, the Athenian constitution would be further destroyed.

Not only did Aeschines anticipate the counter arguments that the defense might use, he attempted to control first the speaker for the defense and then the arrangement of the defense itself. By 330 B.C. the Greek law that each litigant had to conduct his own defense was no longer strictly enforced. Consequently, Ctesiphon would be following accepted legal custom if he chose to have Demosthenes represent him.

Aeschines, however, demanded that Ctesiphon speak in his own defense, but realizing the futility of such a demand, dictated that Demosthenes follow the same order of argument as he himself used. Demosthenes, therefore, could, if he so chose, discount the relatively weak argument that Ctesiphon should speak for himself; but he dared not discount the equitable plea to follow Aeschines' outline. Again, Demosthenes faced a rhetorical dilemma. If he addressed himself to the charges as treated by Aeschines, he would encounter the legal issues first. But confronting the legal technicalities could be disastrous. If, however, Demosthenes used an arrangement other than Aeschines', the jury could only conclude that Demosthenes did so to baffle them, as Aeschines had predicted.

After anticipating and refuting the possible slanders which Demosthenes might raise, Aeschines prolonged his harangue with copious doses of invective interspersed with more commonplaces on general themes, and then concluded.

Such were the arguments which Demosthenes had to overcome.

DEMOSTHENES' INTRODUCTION

Determining the boundaries of Demosthenes' introduction is more difficult than such a task would seem. The first eighteen sections usually are considered the proem, and the material from section 18 to section 53 can be labeled the narrative. If, however, we can assume that the opening portion of any speech is that division which secures the benevolence and good will of an audience, then we can, on the basis of the text itself, designate the first fifty-two sections as Demosthenes' introduction. Structurally this portion of the speech forms a coherent unit and can almost be considered as a separate speech in itself. For what actually is accomplished in these sections is apparently a near complete reversal of existing audience attitudes without a single argument directed against the legal issues of the Crown trial. The onus of guilt is switched from Demosthenes and Ctesiphon to Aeschines, and Demosthenes establishes a favorable atmosphere in which to work out his case. This transfer of guilt is accomplished primarily by assertion and implication in the course of Demosthenes' intricate and restrained proem.[1]

Aeschines had attempted to establish commonly held premises concerning the laws and the Athenian constitution as a base for his attack; Demosthenes elects a higher plane of commonality in his first words, "which are a prayer to all our gods and goddesses." The jury is specified as a group of pious men. In section 8 Demosthenes reinforces his appeal to the jurors through their theism by requesting, "that the gods may implant in you the ability to make a decision about this indictment which will prove to be conducive to the good reputation of all of you and the religious piety of each." The gods are briefly introduced again in section 13 and are not mentioned throughout the remainder of the introduction. By picturing himself as one praying, the jurors as pious, and both he and the jurors as responsible to the gods, Demosthenes achieved several crucial argumentative goals.[2] First, he has immediately shifted the mental focus of the jury away from the legal issues. Second, his stance appears higher than compliance with mere human laws, and finally, his prayerful plea invites pity and sympathy rather than antagonism. Most important, however, he defeats the rhetorical dilemma concerning "unrestrained speakers" which Aeschines has posed. Demosthenes could not be accused of unrestraint since the posture of "one at prayer" could be delivered in a solemn, low-key manner. Further, it is incongruous to presume that a pious person is anything less than innocent and lawabiding. Aeschines' charges of impiety, therefore, are turned to Demosthenes' advantage.

Probably the most salient of Aeschines' closing remarks had

[1] Cf. Quintilian, *Institutio Oratoria*, XI.iii.97, for his comment on the "restraint" of Demosthenes' exordium.

[2] *The Oration of Demosthenes On the Crown*, trans. by F. P. Simpson, with a rhetorical commentary by F. P. Donnelly (New York: Fordham University Press, 1941), p. 237. Donnelly notes that εὔνοια, the Greek equivalent for *pietas*, is found as a noun, adjective, or adverb almost 40 times in Demosthenes' address to the jury.

been the request that Demosthenes respond to the charges in the exact order presented by Aeschines. A sudden, but not unskillful, shift of emphasis from the gods to the laws seems to have served to distract the jurors from Aeschines' plea to allow Demosthenes sufficient time to interpret the duties imposed by the juror's oath, i.e., "it means that you should allow each party in the trial to use the type of defense he has chosen and to arrange his defense as he wishes" (section 2). This brief passage is placed in a critical location. It would seem that Demosthenes is tentatively and cautiously exploring the mood of his audience since he shifts immediately to a consideration of Aeschines' "superior position." The explicit statement of the meaning of the juror's oath, nonetheless, does hint that he will follow a pattern different than Aeschines', but Demosthenes does not dwell on this issue.

Instead, the jury is presented with two arguments (3–4) designed to imply that Demosthenes deserves pity. Even if some jury members were reluctant to allow Demosthenes his own arrangement of arguments, such jurors would be forced to agree that, indeed, "the results of the trial cannot have the same meaning to both of us," and that, "it is a natural characteristic of all men to enjoy listening to insults and accusations, but to be offended when they hear men praising themselves." Both statements are generally accepted observations on human nature, neither would ordinarily be disputed. But from the first premise Demosthenes deduces that Aeschines "accuses me from a superior position," thereby implying a degree of inequity. From the second observation he concludes that it is Aeschines' fault that they must listen to his self-praise. The first indication that Demosthenes intends to shift some sort of blame onto Aeschines, therefore, is made explicit.

Within the first four sections, then, a number of threads are begun from which the entire argumentative web will be woven. Demosthenes characterizes himself as one praying, the jury as pious, as well as impartial, and Aeschines as responsible "for whatever the situation itself compels me to say." Demosthenes also suggests that his pattern of defense be allowed. Witness how each of these threads becomes enlarged and rewoven into the speech from section 5 to section 11.

Aeschines had asked that the jurors render a verdict compatible with the constitution and existing laws. Demosthenes, however, requests an "indictment which will prove to be conducive to the good reputation of all of you and the religious piety of each." And again under the camouflage of the juror's favorable mental response to his religious motif he reintroduces the issue of the "arrangement of my defense." His reasoning in this maneuver is somewhat specious (9). Demosthenes' stated reason for temporarily avoiding the indictment is that Aeschines "has spent at least as much of his time in discussing other matters, and mostly in lies about me." It was true that Aeschines had spent the greater part of his speech attacking the life, character, and policy of Demosthenes, but this assertion would not warrant changing the order of arguments. He had to appear able to defend against the legal issues without actually confronting his apparent transgression of the laws until the jury was more favorably disposed. In short, Demosthenes was bluffing.

To cover his bluff Demosthenes introduces two elements designed to divert the audience. In section 10 he pleads:

> If you know me to be the type of man he has accused me of being (for I have never lived anywhere but among you), do not tolerate the sound of my voice, not even if my statesmanship has been brilliantly successful, but stand up and condemn me now.

Not only did no juror stand, but this argument is so phrased that none could. If any Athenian had known Demosthenes to be the scoundrel portrayed by Aeschines, it was his duty to have raised the issue before (see also section 14). Failure to prosecute malefactors was itself punishable by law. Moreover, it is doubtful that Athenians, who prized fairness and equity, would have unfairly silenced a man at the beginning of his defense. Still, the extreme confidence of his offer probably evoked some degree of admiration from the jury.

The second diversionary element displays Demosthenes' understanding of his audience. In section 11 he overtly previews his procedure, covertly promising to pillory his opponent:

> I will review my policies, the subject of your abusive falsehoods,

and will take up later your loose insults—language worthy of peasant women at a comic festival—if those jurors are willing to listen to them.

Note the strategic points of emphasis. That he intends to consider the charges via his own arrangement is clearly stated for the first time. As a palliative to any objection, however, Demosthenes promises to match insult for insult. The parenthetical invective is an extremely important ploy since it overshadows his statement—"I will review my policies"—and sets a dual theme for his later character assassination. Aeschines' mother will be made a peasant whore, and Aeschines' stage career will serve as the basis for much slander.

Demosthenes' strategy to postpone confronting the legal issues, therefore, is masterfully concealed.

As a direct rejoinder to Aeschines' general premise that "prosecution for violation of laws maintains democracy," Demosthenes clashes with his own specific statements in sections 12–17. First, however, he accepts a version of Aeschines' premise by rephrasing the concept to read, "The city cannot come close to exacting a penalty of the sort demanded by his charges and accusations, if they were, in fact, true." From this premise, Demosthenes proceeds to sketch a portrait of the prosecutor as a man motivated by malice, not by love of justice. As is the case with most of Demosthenes' arguments, this portion of the speech is multifunctional.

The attack on Aeschines' motives provides a framework for using more epithets and innuendoes, i.e., "his theatrical style," "playing the stage part," etc. The attack also furnishes Demosthenes with a logical transition to his narration. The jury is invited to infer that since the motives (11–14) and the tactics (15–16) of Aeschines are questionable, then the accusations (17) also deserve scrutiny. Thirty-five sections of indirect scrutiny are given in the narrative.

Rhetorical theorists have yet to explore narration as a form of gaining communicator credibility or evoking acceptance and belief from an audience—the standard objectives of any argumentative discourse. One need only read the narrative sections of Lysias or the narrative in the Crown speech to observe narrative discourse serving ends other than "relay of information and knowledge of historical facts." For example, the Athenian's just anger at the Thebans is given as the cause for ratifying the Peace of Philocrates in section 20, the initiators of the peace are alleged to have been associates of Aeschines (21), Aeschines' actions and policy are presented as inconsistent (22–24), Demosthenes' seating of the Macedonian ambassadors in the theatre becomes a "main interest" of the State (28).

We can characterize Demosthenes' general method of argument in the narrative as a three-fold process. First, he recounts an historic fact, then he conjecturally adds a course of action that would have been more desirable. Finally, he compares the actual outcome with the more advantageous, although hypothetical, results. This tactic is clearly employed in section 30. The historic fact in this instance is the account of the Athenian ambassadors who "sat in Macedonia three whole months until Philip returned after subjugating all of Thrace." The better course of action would have been "to arrive at the Hellespont and save those places within ten days, perhaps within three or four, by administering the oaths before they were seized by Philip." The third phase of the process is the conjectural comparison between what actually happened, i.e., Philip now has "the Peace and the territory," and what *could have happened*, i.e., "if our representatives were there, he would not have laid a hand on the places."

An intriguing variation on the tripartite formula occurs in sections 35–41. The historic data are Aeschines' proposals, the conjectured course of action is replaced by the actual, undesirable results of Aeschines' counsel, but the conclusion via comparison remains:

> Of course you feel sorrow at what has happened, Aeschines, and pity the Thebans; you have an estate in Bœotia and farm Bœotians' land; of course I rejoice, whose person was demanded immediately by the destroyer of Thebes (41).

A workable strategy for countering anticipatory refutation can be learned by studying the concluding sections of Demosthenes' introduction. Aeschines, it will be remembered, had forecast that Demosthenes would attempt to brand him as a "friend of Alexander." Aeschines had also warned the jurors to remember that he had brought the suit while Philip was still alive. Demosthenes, however, seizes the phrase, "friendship of Alexander," and expands the antonym:

> I reproach you with the friendship of Alexander? Where did you get it from? How did you deserve it? I would not call you—I am not insane—the guest of Philip or the friend of Alexander, unless one should also call farm hands or any other kind of hireling guests and friends of their employers. Before, I called you the hireling of Philip and now, the hireling of Alexander, as do all of these here (51–52).

Demosthenes' rejoinder, of course, has no logical validity. If one explores the first fifty sections, no evidence is advanced to establish the assertion, "Aeschines took bribes." Instead, rhetorical validity, the acceptance of an assertion by an audience as probable, renders the "hireling" argument successful. It is worthwhile to examine Demosthenes' method in achieving this rhetorical acceptance.

In section 19 the accepted fact of Philip's "lavishing bribes on the traitors in each city" is stated. Later in section 31 Aeschines is accused of accepting his first bribe while on the Peace embassy. A second allegation is made in section 32, a charge that is plausible since the members of the embassy did remain in Macedonia for an unusually long time. The label of "hireling" is first attached to Aeschines in section 38—immediately after Demosthenes read a decree damaging to Aeschines' peace proposals. Aeschines' acceptance of bribes is made the cause underlying Philip's deception of Athens in section 42. Aeschines' name is the last mentioned in Demosthenes' catalog of infamous traitors (48–49). Finally, with an air of apologetic modesty Demosthenes prepares the jury for his attack by stating, "others of you were, perhaps, irritated at my remarks, I mean those of you who knew that he had been bribed, before I said anything about it" (50).

With such preparation, argument, and timing, then, Demosthenes secured from his audience the acceptance of his claim, "Aeschines is the hireling of Alexander." With this premise obtained, the presumption of causing the Athenian defeat was partially shifted to Aeschines. The presumption of Demosthenes' guilt under the indictment remained.

DEMOSTHENES' ARGUMENTS AGAINST THE INDICTMENT

Outlining Demosthenes' defensive strategy is an exercise in the impossible. Our modern conception of inductive and deductive outlines, based as they are on an Aristotelian logic of inclusion and exclusion, are incapable of encompassing the over-all structure of Demosthenes' defensive maneuvers. Sometimes a temporal pattern emerges, sometimes a causal pattern; some conclusions are implicit. Most, however, are explicit. No single line of reasoning predominates, yet nearly every inferential mode of relationship between premises can be found. In brief, it seems more fruitful to analyze the structure of the Crown speech in terms of separate "scenes" or blocks of persuasion, each of which, at one and the same time, *appears* to be a complete entity in itself, yet, each is intricately dependent on what precedes and exerts control over what is to follow. To examine every such organic unit is beyond the physical limitations of this essay; therefore, only the most characteristic argumentative forms will be assessed.

An excellent instance of reducing the focus of succeeding premises occurs in the first suasive block in which Demosthenes reviews the record of his foreign policy (61 and after). He asks first what Athens should have done to counter the treachery of Philip. Then he narrows the scope of his query to "what should a statesman have done?" He answers by identifying his policy with that of his countrymen:

> Therefore, the only choice, and the necessary choice, left to you was justly to oppose all his unjust actions against you. This course you took from the beginning, naturally and fittingly, this course I proposed and advised in the time of my political activity. I admit it. What should I have done (69)?

Here again Demosthenes' seemingly innocent questioning is designed to elicit a host of favorable reactions from his jury. The unspoken, but highly acceptable premise on which this channelized structure rests is, simply, "As Athenians you necessarily and always wanted whatever was best for Athens." Consequently, when, in section 80, Demosthenes enlarges the focus of his comments to encompass the Athenians again he becomes the individual who merely helped them do what Athenians would have done anyway:

> Afterwards I was responsible for sending out all the naval expeditions which saved the Chersonese, Byzantium, and the rest of our allies. As a result of these actions, you received the noblest rewards from those who received your help: praise, glory, honors, crowns, gratitude.

If one were to diagram the argumentative form of Demosthenes' premises regarding his foreign policy, an hourglass shape would emerge. At the top and bottom of the hourglass are the premises and statements wherein Demosthenes associates his actions with those of the Athenians, but at the stricture of the hourglass Demosthenes speaks only of himself. One critic has described the "foreign policy" section in this way:

> The contrast, Athens and Greece, Athens and Philip, the dilemma and disjunctive reasoning, the forceful refrain "What was I to do," the echoing of significant words, κωλύω and ἐναντιοῦμαι, the comprehensive grasp of Greek history and of Philip's career, the imagination in concreteness, detail, and comparison, the proofs in climactic order, the constant and alternating contact with judges and adversary, the motives for emotions, proud joy in contrast with the fate of others, in exultant joy that Philip was outrivaled in honor, and the just anger at the catalog of Philip's aggressions, these with other traits are excellences of persuasion in evidence here.[3]

A second suasive component that merits discussion is Demosthenes' exposition of his naval reforms (102–109). Aeschines had charged Demosthenes with accepting bribes and pandering to the wealthy leaders of several Hellenic states. Nowhere in the Crown speech does Demosthenes *directly deny accepting bribes;* instead, he creates a predisposition of probable innocence by interludes such as the naval reform account. Masking his strategy under a narrative exposition of his domestic policy, a policy established twenty years before the Crown trial, Demosthenes presents himself as a statesman who was vitally concerned with helping the poor at the risk of offending the wealthy. Observe for example how Demosthenes insinuates that he is above accepting bribes:

[3] Donnelly, p. 265.

And yet, how much money do you think I was offered by those in the highest tax brackets not to submit this law for passage, or, if not that, at least to let it be suspended while its legality was being appealed? Men of Athens, I would hesitate to tell you how much it was. But their attempt was reasonable (103).

This passage provokes even the modern reader's curiosity. How much money was offered? by whom? And yet, the naval reform law had been passed, thereby implying Demosthenes' incorruptibility. Instead of allowing the audience to infer that he should be praised for his reform measures, he specifies what he wants and why: "Moreover, I deserve praise for this, that I chose the policies which brought praise and honor and power to the city" (108). His demand, in its context, appears just and reasonable.

Demosthenes' defensive strategy against the legal issues (111–123) forms another suasive unit. The theory undergirding his refutation is simple: amplify the nature of law, establish favorable precedents, and be indignant. Against the law of accountability he asks:

What law is so thoroughly inhuman and unjust as to cause an official who gave some of his personal property and performed a humane and generous act to be robbed of gratitude, to be exposed to malicious accusers, and to put these in control of the accounts he submitted? There is no such law (112).

Essentially the same strategy is apparent in his rejoinder to the illegality of proclaiming a Crown in the theatre:

But, for heaven's sake, Aeschines, are you so imperceptive and so stupid that you cannot grasp the fact that the gift of a Crown causes the same pride in its recipient wherever it is proclaimed? And that the proclamation in the theatre assists the purposes of the donors? All who hear the proclamation are encouraged to serve their city and they praise those who confer the favor more than its recipient (120).

The manifest weakness of his position is again masked by Demosthenes' two favorite gambits when defending against a stronger argument: (1) attack Aeschines or Philip or both,[4]

---

[4] Cf. Isocrates, *Antidosis* 21–23. Isocrates blames Athenian juries for neglecting the merits of a trial and, instead, attending to the pilloring of an opponent's private life.

and (2) identify with the jurors so that an attack on Demosthenes is an attack on Athens. Demosthenes slips away from the charges of illegality by an intensive personal attack on Aeschines (121 and following) and immediately moves toward increased identification with his audience by taunting, "Watch out that you don't prove to be the enemy of these citizens here, while you claim to be mine" (125).

This two-fold shift of focus controls the next two major elements in the speech. After playing the melody in sections 121–125, he embellishes the attack on Aeschines in the succeeding twenty sections. Then he returns to his role as an Athenian statesman (169 and following). Following the extended quotation from his own speech after the fall of Elateia, he establishes himself not only as an Athenian statesman, but as Athens' bravest leader. Witness the climactic build in the following premises:

> All, together, praised my advice; no one opposed it. I did not speak, but fail to propose measures; I did not propose measures, but fail to serve as ambassador; I did not serve as ambassador, but fail to persuade the Thebans; from beginning to end I persevered and faced, without reserve, the dangers threatening the city (179).

It was necessary that Demosthenes align himself with his audience to evoke sympathy; it was equally necessary to establish himself as a superior Athenian to counteract the presumption of guilt from leading Athens to defeat. Aeschines had given six characteristics of a true statesman and found Demosthenes wanting in all but speaking ability. Demosthenes, however, simultaneously avoiding the slightest hint of antagonism with his jury and maintaining his identification with his Athenian audience, builds toward his conception of the role of a statesman throughout the entire speech. Then, in section 246 he defines "everything for which a statesman is accountable." His concept differs markedly from that advanced by the prosecution:

> To see situations as they arise and to inform the rest of the citizens. This I did. To confine within the smallest possible limits, whenever they arise, hesitation, reluctance to act, ignorance, personal ambition—those necessary and inherent defects of all

free governments—and to convert these qualities into concord and friendship and the impulse to do what must be done. All this I did. . . .

Demosthenes concludes, on the basis of his definition, that, "our city was not defeated, insofar as I am representative of it" (247). But the ultimate conclusion to Demosthenes' reasoning in which he exonerates himself for the Athenian defeat is the epigram in section 290, " 'Never to fail, always to succeed, is the privilege of the gods.' " The implication was clear: a statesman cannot be held legally responsible for the uncontrollable failure of his policy. The jury agreed.

In brief summary, then, we can say that Demosthenes argued from theism to gain a hearing, from his successful policies to gain a predisposition of respect, from his honors as Athenian honors to gain identification, from his opponent to gain an alternate scapegoat, and finally, he argued from definition to establish himself as a statesman who did what he could and failed only because fate so decreed.

Demosthenes' Use of Language

by Galen O. Rowe

The pre-eminence of the oration *On the Crown* was nobly attested by Demosthenes' only peer in ancient oratory, Cicero, who said that no man could ask for greater eloquence (*Orator* 133). The speech represents one of history's rare moments when theory and practice, beauty and utility each reaches its optimum and at the same time complements the other. *On the Crown* is a carefully chiseled and polished work of art; but nowhere are we allowed to forget that it is also a deadly weapon forged to be used in forensic combat. Demosthenes, so the story goes, regarded the composition of his speeches in the light of a sculptor carefully working each detail into sharp relief. He avoided speaking extemporaneously whenever possible. But when asked the three main requirements for effective oratory, he replied, "Delivery, delivery, delivery." We cannot imagine that Demosthenes, the orator, judged the merits of his address solely on the basis of its adherence to rhetorical teaching. That it faithfully followed any preconceived æsthetic criteria was of secondary importance. The acid test was the courtroom, the final critics the jury. The style in *On the Crown* was a means of persuasion. Language, phrasing, and figurations of speech all played their parts to gain for the orator the vindication of his name and the humiliation of his enemy.

The language of *On the Crown* is the Attic dialect spoken by Demosthenes' opponent, Aeschines, and other notable orators of the day, such as Lysias and Isocrates. But unlike the vocabularies of his contemporaries, Demosthenes' language encompasses a range of words extending from the basest epithets to the loftiest expression of poetry. Abstract and concrete words thrive in the same context. In order to be effective, however, language requires the diligent control of the orator. The words must be appropriate to their surroundings. In this respect one thinks of the jarring effect of Andocides' poetic expressions in their rather mundane contexts. Such is not the case with Demosthenes, whose words seldom seem out of harmony with the ideas they are meant to express. One manifestation of his control is the recurrent associations built around each of his main figures—himself, Aeschines, Philip, and the city of Athens. Through the use of the same word, the same epithet or type of epithet, and the same imagery, Demosthenes fashions the protagonists in his oration in such a way as to win our sympathy, excite our imagination, or provoke our disgust.

The Greek word *eunoia*, translated either as "good will" or "patriotism," occurs with its adverbial and adjectival forms over forty times. Winning the benevolence of the audience was one of the main functions to be performed by the proem of a speech. Demosthenes observes this function in his solemn opening prayer for good will. But instead of discarding the expression, after it has served its purpose, he reiterates it in the main body of the speech (section 199). Moreover, "good will" or "patriotism" becomes a touchstone which the orator applies to himself and to his opponent. Demosthenes was always well-minded and patriotic toward Athens (173, 320), but Aeschines' attitude was never that of a just and patriotic citizen (198). As a result of Demosthenes' policies the inhabitants of the Chersonese and Byzantium bestowed honor and good will upon the Athenians (94); Aeschines' policies never brought good will to Athens (311). Aeschines made no contribution either of money or of patriotic zeal to the state (312), while patriotic zeal guided Demosthenes' actions (286). Demosthenes constantly assures his audience that patriotism is an attitude basic to his relationship with them; but Aeschines is carefully excluded from this association. He was rejected by the Council of the Areopagus for being a traitor and opposed (in Greek *kako-noun*, literally, "evil-minded") to Athens' interests (136). Through the repetition of the word in the same frame of reference Demosthenes at once pre-empts the sympathy of his audience and alienates his opponent.

The opprobious epithets heaped on Aeschines are strongly reminiscent of comedy. Names of animals or proverbs describing animal traits were favorite expressions of the playwright Aristophanes. In the oration Aeschines is called a "sly beast" (162, the Sicilian word for "fox"); his cowardly behavior is epitomized in the proverb, "you lead the life of a rabbit" (263). The diminutive, another comic device, is applied to Aeschines: he is a "paltry man" (242, one word in Greek, something like "mannequin"). Also important to the bizarre atmosphere, which comedy seeks to create, are unusual words and neologisms. Aristophanes' strange compounds, like "Cloudcuckooland," are almost matched by Demosthenes' descriptive of his opponent—"idle babbler" (127, literally, "picker-up-of-seeds") or "court hack" (127, literally "hack-of-the-market-place").

Aeschines' early career as an actor of the tragic stage comes in for special ridicule. "Third-rate actor" or "bad actor" (same word in Greek) is an epithet found five times in the oration. The insult is reinforced by descriptives like "stage monkey," "rustic Oinomaos" (242), and "tragic Theokrines" (313). The abuse cast upon Aeschines' acting ability is carefully planned. His real forte, Demosthenes suggests, is comedy, not tragedy:

> . . . you brought no shame, by Zeus, on any of your former occupations by your life afterwards, but hired yourself out to the actors Simukas and Sokrates, the famous "Groaners," and played your small roles collecting, from the audience, like a fruit seller from other people's farms, figs and grapes and olives, getting more from this source than from your dramatic contests, in which your troupe engaged at the risk of its life. For there was a truceless and never-ending war between you and the spectators, who inflicted upon you so many wounds that you naturally ridicule as cowards those who never faced such risks (262).

This passage will call to mind how the tragedian Euripides is transformed into a comic character in the plays of Aristophanes.

Judged by itself, the ridicule of Aeschines' acting talents is devastating. But Demosthenes will not leave it at that. Constant mention of Aeschines' dramatic career leads to the additional suggestion that in the present lawsuit "he is playing a stage part, piling up charges and jokes and abuse much after the events" (15). Aeschines screams every kind of filthy name at Demosthenes, "like a comic reveler from a wagon" (122). Aeschines criticizes his opponent's words and gestures (126, 232). In short, he is a "counterfeit statesman" (242), more concerned with making a rhetorical exhibition and a display of voice than with securing the punishment for actual crimes. Demosthenes, through a pattern of comic epithets and descriptives, works to discredit Aeschines in the eyes of the jury. The language of comedy changes his adversary from the tragic hero to the comic buffoon who makes a flop of all his roles and who speaks without conviction or regard for the truth.

Other recurrent patterns of language are to be found in the similes and metaphors. One type of imagery is that of buying and selling; its presence in the oration is remarkable, since it presents a reply by Demosthenes to an elaborate simile of his opponent. Aeschines had declared it necessary to review Demosthenes' conduct with the same objectivity as an accountant; and, when the debits are found to erase all of the credits, any favorable presuppositions about his merits must be abandoned (227). Demosthenes adroitly turns this simile to his advantage by adding up the balance and finding it in his favor (230, 231). But the response does not end at that point; Demosthenes has his own comparison of accounting to fit his opponent: Aeschines is like a balance verging toward the side of monetary gain (298). The orator stresses the idea that Aeschines has sold his loyalty to the enemy (38, 41, 47, 49, 50, 138). Philip is portrayed as the buyer in the market place ready to snap up any who would desert the side of Athens (239).

The charge of moral corruption is enhanced and strengthened by imagery of physical pollution and disease. Demosthenes refers to his opponents as "polluted," each of whom "crippled his own country," and "measured his happiness by his belly" (296). Early in the speech he describes his efforts on Athens' behalf and attributes their lack of success to the fact that "the cities were diseased; their political leaders were corrupting themselves by taking bribes" (45). The same imagery of physical corruption describes Aeschines:

> A measure is being discussed which the Athenians think supports their interests; Aeschines is silent. There was resistance, and something unexpected happened; Aeschines is there, like ruptures and strains which afflict the body when it is stricken by some disease (198).

Aeschines has never tendered any "helpful" (literally "healthy") advice (23). Instead, he is like a doctor who, while his patients are ill, refuses to prescribe a remedy, but, when their funeral rites are being observed, joins the procession explaining in detail what the victim should have done to escape death (243). When there is need for constructive counsel, Aeschines remains in the background "like a festering sore" (307). He has spewed upon Demosthenes "the garbage of his own villainy" (50). Aeschines' illness, Demosthenes suggests, is a feverish madness which requires a dose of hellebore (121). The imagery of physical corruption reaches its fitting climax in Demosthenes' concluding prayer:

> I pray to all the gods that they refuse assent to this desire but rather implant in these men a better mind and a better spirit; if they are beyond cure, may they, and they alone, be quickly and utterly destroyed, . . . (324)

In describing his personal role in Athens' confrontation with Philip, Demosthenes adopts the metaphor of the soldier at his post. Early in the speech he states that he took his "position" (62) in government at a time when all the Greeks were divided against each other and ignorant of the growing danger of Philip's domination. After Philip had captured Elateia and the leading Athenian statesmen were unable to offer advice for the city's protection, Demosthenes alone "did not desert the post that patriotism required in time of danger" (173). Anticipating the objection that he assumed too much responsibility, Demosthenes replies, "I was at my post in each of these spheres"

(221). Like a true soldier, Demosthenes used his policies and acts as a shield in front of Attica (300). The metaphor is particularly important when we remember that Aeschines had accused Demosthenes of cowardice (*Against Ctesiphon* 175); but the orator also uses it as a means of sharpening the distinction between himself and Aeschines. Contrasting the facility of Aeschines' collaboration with Philip and the difficulty of his own efforts, he points out, "it is always easier and safer to be a hireling in the service of your enemies than to choose the post of your protector in the field of politics" (138). Throughout the oration the metaphor refers to Demosthenes, but in the concluding lines the orator provides an ironic touch by applying it to his opponent:

> But when that unfortunate defeat was suffered, and there was a call no longer for advisers but for men who would submit to orders, who were ready to harm their country for pay, who were willing to court another, then you and each of your comrades were at your post, . . . (320)

In the above quoted passage there is an unmistakable allusion to the situation in Athens after the capture of Elateia (cf. 173) when Demosthenes was the only citizen to answer his country's call for guidance. This time the call is out for flatterers and men servile to Philip; Aeschines and his comrades are in position.

The weather images associated with Philip are a clear indication of Demosthenes' respect for Athens' long-time foe. Although the orator remarks amply on Philip's wickedness, his treachery and the swift, unexpected nature of his movements receive special emphasis. Philip's capture of Elateia posed an immediate threat to Athens, and had it not been for the resistance of the Thebans, he would have swept down upon the city "like a river in torrent" (153). Weather imagery is again employed when Demosthenes' policy caused the danger of Philip's encroachments to pass by "like a cloud" (188). Demosthenes hesitates to recall an incident before Philip's final and absolute conquest, which has caused the past to vanish as though "obliterated . . . by a flood" (214). The association of Philip with natural elements reaches its peak in the following passage:

If the lightning that struck us was too great not only for us but for the rest of Greece as well, what were we to do? It is just as if one were to blame for the shipwreck the owner who has taken every precaution, has equipped his ship with everything he believes will ensure its safety, but then the ship meets with a storm and its tackling weakens or is completely ruined. But I was not a captain of a ship, one might say (as I was not a general either), nor did I control fate; rather, fate controlled everything (194).

Two ideas in this passage call for elaboration. The first is that Philip is portrayed in his role as lightning and storm—instruments of destiny over which human effort and wisdom have little control. The orator repeats this idea; and, in so doing, he bestows upon the historical events the significance of tragedy. Secondly, there is the unmistakable inclusion of the ship-of-state imagery, which figures prominently in Greek poetry and drama. It is echoed later in the oration when Demosthenes declares that Aeschines by failing to demonstrate loyalty to Athens "does not ride at the same anchor with the people" (281). The portrayal of Athens as the ship and Philip as the storm vividly projects the struggle to cosmic proportions. Though Athens was destined to lose the war, it remained within her power to preserve her dignity and to assert her moral choice— it is in the expression of this view that the language of Demosthenes reaches the heights of tragic poetry.

I wish to make a rather paradoxical assertion. Do not be amazed, by Zeus and the gods, if I say something extreme; rather, let everyone examine what I say with good will. If the outcome was entirely clear, and everyone knew about it beforehand, and you were predicting it, Aeschines, shouting at the top of your voice—you who did not utter a word—not even in those circumstances should the city have backed off from its course, if in fact it was concerned for its reputation or its forefathers or the future (199).

Recurrent words, epithets, and images are indicative of the orator's almost total control of language; but, what is more important, they contribute to the persuasive power of the oration. Through the frequent repetition of the same word Demosthenes implants in the minds of his audience a persistent concept

difficult to refuse. Throughout the speech Demosthenes re-
minds his audience that his relationship to them is, and should
be, mutual good will. Three recurrent patterns of language are
employed for Aeschines' characterization: his venality is under-
scored by imagery of buying and selling; his ineffectual hypoc-
risy receives emphasis as Demosthenes caricatures his career on
the tragic stage with comic words and epithets; finally, his corruption is made vivid by similes and metaphors of pollution
and disease. Demosthenes, on the other hand, represents himself as the soldier, who refused to abandon his post even in the
darkest hours of crisis. The language assumes a poetic quality
when dealing with the history of Athens' unsuccessful conflict
with Philip. Through weather imagery and the ship-of-state
simile he ennobles the defeat to which his policies had led. At
least three purposes are assisted through the selection and re-
currence of language—the good will of the audience, their ap-
proval for Demosthenes' policies, and the alienation of Aeschines.

The intensity and range of Demosthenes' language would
lose much of its effectiveness without the dynamic flexibility of
his phrasing. His achievement in this regard can be determined
best by comparison with the three most influential stylists in
Greek prose—Gorgias, Lysias, and Isocrates. Gorgias had bequeathed to his successors in oratory a sense for balance and
contrast through the use of antithesis. But the constant juxta-
posing of two opposite ideas becomes trite and monotonous
with its metronome-like regularity. Lysias excelled in his ability
to describe events by means of simple clauses. His oratory,
though never dull, was nevertheless incapable of soaring to the
heights of eloquence. Isocrates perfected the complicated expressive structure which represents the periodic style. The danger in using this vehicle of expression lies in the tendency toward
artificiality and intricacy where they are neither desirable nor
warranted. Demosthenes' regard for oratory as a means to an
end rather than as an end in itself saves him from excess in any
of the three modes of expression. His style absorbs the Gorgian,
Lysian, and Isocratean traits, while at the same time it makes
them uniquely his own.

Antithesis, although it had always been a common means of

expression in the Greek language, received special attention from Gorgias. Later rhetoricians were to differentiate various types of antithesis, and it will help to consider them at this point in the discussion. Antithesis may consist merely of words, such as "the rich and prosperous man should give to the poor and needy man." Again, there may be antithesis of thought but not of language: "I nursed him when he was sick, but he has been the cause of the greatest evils to me." The perfected type, however, contains both polarity of terminology and of meaning: "It is not just for my opponent to have possessions and be rich, while I have parted with my property and live as a beggar." This last type Gorgias cultivated to an excessive degree. He increased the antithetical effect by adding rhythm and rhyme. Artificial effects, characteristic of the Gorgian antithesis, tended to deprive the expression of the spontaneity and freedom necessary for judicial oratory. Orators of the courts, like Lysias and Demosthenes, employed the Gorgian antithesis; but more often antithesis was the basis for an extended unit of thought, which we may call the antithetical "period."

A striking instance of the Gorgian antithesis is the following passage (265):

> You taught school, I attended school.
> You initiated people, I was an initiate.
> You were a minor clerk, I was a member of the Assembly.
> You were a minor actor, I was a spectator.
> You were hissed off the stage, I joined in the hissing.
> Your policies supported our enemy, mine, our country.

In this example it is possible to see that the Gorgian antithesis demands a large measure of similarity between the contrasting elements. First, there is uniformity of word order in all six of the groups—subject, verb, and object or predicate noun. There is also similarity in the parts of speech; the subjects for the first five statements are personal pronouns, "you" and "I." A similarity of length (more so in the Greek) exists; both elements in each antithesis above have nearly the same number of words. The actual contrast may be provided merely by a change in inflection, as in the second one where the verb is changed from the active voice of the first element to the passive voice of the second. Or it may be a change in one word, as in the first comparison where "taught" is changed to "attended." Thus the danger of monotony is a very real one. But in our example the danger is avoided. The passage provides an antithetical summary to Demosthenes' comparison between the public lives of Aeschines and of himself. It is therefore appropriate as a conclusion to this section of the oration. Moreover, while each of the antitheses is tightly symmetrical and concise, there is a progressive development in the passage as a whole. It follows a chronological sequence beginning with the early private lives of each individual and culminating in their mature capacities as statesmen at Athens. By using this form Demosthenes emphasizes that Aeschines' traitorous activities in government were the natural result of his consistently ignominious private life, while his own contributions were the outcome of a life in harmony with the best Athenian traditions.

As a rule, Demosthenes avoids the constrictive balance associated with the Gorgian mode. A contemporary writer of comedy, Timocles, calls him "a fire-eating hater of literature who never uttered an antithesis in his life." Indeed, it sometimes appears as though the orator deliberately avoids symmetry where it would be easily employed, as in this example:

> The pleasurable side is given to Aeschines, the part which irritates nearly everybody is left for me (4).

The two contrasting ideas of the statement do not have equally contrasting language. From Gorgias one might expect something like this:

> That which affords pleasure is given to him, while that which provokes anger is left to me.

Inconcinnity, or purposeful disharmony, particularly in the use of antithesis, was a prominent feature in the writing of the Greek historian Thucydides, and some critics have felt that Demosthenes borrowed this technique from him. Demosthenes' style, however, hardly resembles that of Thucydides in other respects, so that the likelihood of the historian's influence is not great. A more valid reason is that the constricting nature of the Gorgian antithesis is not usually compatible with the total Demosthenic expression, which flows in an expansive and flexible manner. It is for this reason that antithesis in the oration *On the Crown* occurs most often in the periodic structures where each of the two opposed ideas is refined and elaborated through subordinate clauses. The following example will serve to illustrate:

> When our city was free to choose the best policy and a prize for patriotism was open to all, I advised the strongest measures and all our affairs were conducted by my decrees and laws and embassies; no one of your group was anywhere to be seen except when you felt a need to discredit my proposals. But when that unfortunate defeat was suffered, and there was a call no longer for advisers but for men who would submit to orders, who were ready to harm their country for pay, who were willing to court another, then you and each of your comrades were at your post, fine, important people with handsome stallions. I was powerless, I admit it, but I was more patriotic than you (320).

Certain dominant contrasts appear in this period, such as the contrast between the past before the battle of Chæronea and the time after the Athenian defeat, between those who contended for the prize of patriotism and those who sought to harm their country for pay, and between those who were ready to advise and those who would submit to orders; but nowhere is the polarity allowed to become rigid or to control the thought. It is to be noticed that Demosthenes does not place the opposites side by side, and that he inserts certain elements of inconcinnity which prevent the expression from attaining perfect symmetry and balance. The following outline from the previous passage will help to make the structure clear:

1a When our city was free . . .

1b and a prize for patriotism was open to all,

1 I advised . . .

2a But when that unfortunate defeat was suffered,

2b and there was a call . . . for men

    2b$_1$ who would submit to orders,

$2b_2$ who were ready to harm . . .

$2b_3$ who were willing to court . . .

2 Then you . . . were at your post, . . .

3 I was powerless, . . .

The subordinate clauses *1a* and *2a*, *1b* and *2b*, *1* and *2* are antithetical to each other; but in each case they are separated by two intervening clauses. Notice also that *2b* is prevented from being symmetrical to *1b* by the addition of three relative clauses ($2b_1$, $2b_2$, $2b_3$). The entire passage is strongly antithetical, but it manages to be expansive rather than concise, flexible rather than rigid. It moves with the freedom characteristic of Demosthenic prose, yet contains sufficient balance and proportion. Antithesis in *On the Crown* is an example of the genius of Demosthenes in adapting to his own style an outstanding trait of his predecessor.

The most common expressive structure in the oration is the simple clause, by which is meant the presentation of a complete thought with little or no subordination. Lysias, whose appeal was largely the result of his ability to describe an event or a situation, had made the clause ideal for narration. Its unique advantage is rapidity and clarity in presenting the necessary background material of the oration. In the hands of a skilled orator it can also contain considerable animation. One is reminded of the artist, who with a few strokes of charcoal can capture and bring to life all the essential details of a scene. Observe how Demosthenes sketches the scene in Athens following the news of Elateia's defeat:

> It was evening. Someone came reporting to the Prytanes that Elateia had been captured. Some of them got up immediately, in the middle of dinner, and began to drive out the merchants in the stalls around the market place and to burn the wicker booths; others had the generals summoned and called for the trumpeter. The city was filled with confusion. At dawn of the next day, the Prytanes summoned the Council to the Council chamber, while you proceeded to the Assembly. The whole people was already seated before the Council started their business and passed a motion. Afterwards, when the Council came and

the Prytanes reported the information they had received, they brought in the messenger and he spoke. Then the herald asked, "Who wishes to speak?" No one came forward (169).

With an economy of means Demosthenes vividly depicts the urgency of the situation. The paratactic clauses, loosely connected, underscore the flurry of activity culminating neatly in the request of the herald: "Who wishes to speak?" Demosthenes proves that he is able to rival Lysias in using the simple clause for narration. But to the clarity of Lysias' narration he adds another virtue—force. His simple clauses often appear in groups whose members are closely synonymous, like this example:

a Further, the whole of the Peloponnese was in dissension,
b the most bitter enemies of the Spartans were not strong enough to destroy them,
c those who formerly ruled through the influence of the Spartans were not in control of their cities,
d but there was a kind of strife-ridden confusion among these peoples and among the rest of the Greeks which did not admit of settlement (18).

By means of four clauses Demosthenes emphasizes the divisions which prevailed in Greece. He prevents the emphasis from seeming ponderous by the artistic arrangement of the clauses; *a* and *d* say essentially the same thing, although *d*, as the concluding member, is longer and more fullsome than *a*. Clauses *b* and *c* identify the two main factions in the dissension. The thought in the combined group moves from the general to the specific and from the specific back to the general. Emphasis is achieved through the careful modulation of synonymy.

Although critics, both ancient and modern, have disagreed about Demosthenes' merits in other matters, they have unanimously acclaimed the richness and force of his periodicity. Definitions of the oratorical period in antiquity tended to be vague and conflicting, a fact which can be explained by the almost unlimited variety of structural patterns found in the periods of ancient prose. It is possible, however, to establish certain characteristics. The first is length; most periodic structures exceed one hundred words. Secondly, the period is characterized by extensive subordination which may attain four degrees. The subordinate clauses, or "cola," as they are called in this context, may assume a variety of forms, such as relative or temporal clauses or conditions. Finally, the period must be so constructed as to permit the thought to develop and grow through the cola until it reaches completion. Few orators were able to fulfill all these requirements on the grand scale of Isocrates and Demosthenes; and, although Isocrates was perhaps the greater artist, Demosthenes' unique achievement was a period with strength as well as beauty. *On the Crown,* revealing the orator at the height of his power and control over expression, contains some of the most famous periodic structures in Greek prose. The opening statement of the proem is a fine example:

> My first words, men of Athens, are a prayer to all our gods and goddesses that in this trial I may depend on as much good will from you as I have continually maintained toward our city and toward all of you; secondly—something which concerns your piety and your reputation to the highest degree—I pray the gods to implant in your minds the thought that you should not let my opponent advise you of the manner in which you should listen to me (for that would be harsh) but that you be guided by the laws and your oath, which imposes the special obligation upon you to listen to both parties in the same manner (1).

A brief glance back over the period will reveal the variety of its components. Parallelism, parenthesis, subordination, and expansion play their separate parts in the progression and completion of the thought. The design may be more clearly perceived with the aid of this outline of part of the preceding passage:

a My first words . . .

  a1 that in this trial I may depend on as much . . .

  a2 as I have continually maintained . . .

b secondly—something which . . . —I pray . . .

    b1 that you should not . . . the manner

      b1' in which you should listen—for that would be harsh—

    b2 but that you be guided by the laws and your oath,

      b2' which imposes

In spite of the complexity of this period, unity is imposed by the simple base, consisting of the parallel cola *a* and *b*. Each of the two cola contains one subordinate parallelism (*a1a2* and *b1b2*). The impression of enlargement is served by increased subordination in the second group (*b*). *Colon b* contains an anticipatory gloss ("—something which . . . —"), and *b1* and *b2* each has a subordinate "colon." The structure harmonizes with the meaning and purpose of the period. Since the opening statement is a prayer, it possesses dignity and moves at a solemn pace. Through the use of the simple base Demosthenes permits the thought to be expansive without frivolity. The increased subordination and the parenthesis between *b1'* and *b2* ("—for that would be harsh—") prevents an increase in momentum.

The period is not a mode of expression to be employed with great frequency. Even the Athenians with their insatiable love of speeches could not have been expected to follow its circuitous path, however aesthetically satisfying, without respite. If constantly employed in judicial or political oratory, it could have the disastrous effect of wearying the jury. Moreover, when the period is used, it must convey an idea worthy of its elaborate structure. Demosthenes' awareness of these conditions saves him from succumbing to pettiness. With him the period is an instrument of heroic expression; it is reserved for those moments of emotional sublimity which only he knew how to create.

What was the only policy for a statesman at Athens—for this makes all the difference—to advise or propose, a statesman who knew that our country, throughout its history up to the day he himself ascended the speaker's platform, always fought for the first rank in honor and reputation, and had spent more men and money for the honor and benefit of all than the rest of the

Greeks had spent in their own behalf, a statesman who saw that Philip, with whom was our struggle, had had his eye knocked out, his collarbone broken, his hand and his leg maimed for the sake of preserving his rule, and was ready to sacrifice any part of his body which fortune would take, so that he could live in honor and glory (66–67)?

The emotional grandeur of Demosthenes' periodic structure is exemplified by this passage. The period is stated as a rhetorical question, but there is also much narrative in it. Four parties and their participation in the struggle are enumerated—Demosthenes as a statesman in Athens, Athens as the champion of Greece, and Philip as the enemy to their combined interests. Lofty, abstract words and graphic, concrete words both find their places in the structure. Through the graphic narrative we are caused to visualize Demosthenes ascending the speaker's platform and the battle-scarred body of Philip, but these pictures, in turn, find their meaning in such abstract terms as "honor and reputation," "honor and benefit," and "fortune." Because of Demosthenes' mastery of expression all of the elements in the period have cohesion. The thought progresses through subordination, parallelism, and antithesis to its completion in the final two words: "honor and glory." As is the case with Demosthenes' style elsewhere, in this period there is an evolution of thought from the real to the ideal and from the particular to the universal.

"Periodic" is the adjective used to describe Demosthenes' prose; but instances of the elaborate subordination of a single, complex thought are relatively few in his masterpiece. There are, however, valid reasons for the use of this descriptive. *On the Crown* presents not only some of the finest periods in Greek prose, it also conveys in every passage the impression of movement and expansion in the periodic manner. This impression may be accounted for in part by the variety of clauses which move easily from antithesis to parallelism to subordination. But the main explanation is *sensus suspensio,* or suspension of meaning. By this technique details, which are essential for the completion of the thought, are withheld until the end of the clause, for example:

Philip, who appropriated Eubœa, who prepared to make it a
fortress against Attica, who attempted to get control of Megara,
who seized Oreos, who razed Porthmos, who set up the tyrants
Philistides in Oreos and Kleitarchos in Eretria, who subjugated
the Hellespont, who besieged Byzantium, who destroyed some
Greek cities and restored exiles to others—in these actions was
Philip doing wrong, and breaking treaties, and disrupting the
Peace or not (71)?

A succession of ten relative clauses enumerating Philip's ag-
gressions precedes the main statement. The subordination is
simple, attaining only the first degree; but there are in the passage elements suggestive of the amplitude of the period. The
first such element is the protracted list of Philip's activities.
More than a list of statements, it presents a panorama of history. Although the events described are similar, Demosthenes
has chosen to focus each in a separate clause thereby enhanc-
ing its significance. A second indication of amplitude is the
combination of the general and the particular. There are three
levels of meaning in the passage—the particular aggression
against an individual city (i.e., "razed Porthmos"), the general
activity of aggression (i.e., "destroyed some Greek cities"),
and the moral significance of aggression (i.e., "Philip doing
wrong"). The movement of the passage progresses in the periodic manner. There is syntactical progression, as the series of
relative clauses at the beginning causes the reader to look forward to the completion of the thought. Chronological progression is also present; the events are described in historical sequence. Finally, there is progression in levels of meaning·from
the particular attack on an individual city to the general destruction of Greek cities to the moral significance of the combined acts.

Another example of *sensus suspensio* uses the condition and
the participle for the preliminary subordination:

If the outcome was entirely clear, and everyone knew about it
beforehand, and you were predicting it, Aeschines, shouting at
the top of your voice—you who did not utter a word—not even
in those circumstances should the city have backed off from its
course (199).

As in the passage quoted above, a progression of thought occurs in the groups of conditional clauses; but in this instance
the ideas move from the general to the specific rather than vice
versa. The suspension of meaning is intensified by the partici-
pial and parenthetic elaborations of Aeschines in the third condition.

Demosthenes knows a variety of ways by which to tantalize
his listeners' attention—subordinate clauses of all kinds, inver-
sions, and enumerations like the following:

> On that day, the citizens of Thebes showed all the world three
> qualities of yours which deserve the highest praise: the first is
> your bravery, the second your justice, the third your decent
> behavior (215).

What gives suspension of meaning special effectiveness in Demosthenes' oratory is that with the syntactical progression of
clauses there is also a corresponding progression of thought.

The greatness of *On the Crown* may be attributed to the
fact that it encompasses the three major styles of Greek oratory
—the antithetical structures of Gorgias, the simple clauses perfected by Lysias, and the rotund periodicity of Isocrates. None
of these styles, however, appears as a discrete entity within the
oration; instead, all merge into a single dynamic and flexible
expression. We have shown how Demosthenes maintains flexibility in his antithetical structures through inconcinnity and expansion. He rivals Lysias in recapturing the vitality of historical events through the simple clause; but he surpasses that
orator in forcefulness. In antiquity the attribute which most
distinguished Demosthenes was power. When he assumed into
his style the Isocratean period, famed for its beauty, he made it
an effective instrument of political oratory by providing it with
emotional grandeur and strength. Although the periods of *On
the Crown* are relatively few, the speech as a whole has the
expansiveness and progression of the classic period.

The wide range of Demosthenes' expression may be seen
not only in the architecture of his phrasing but also in the daz-
zling array of his stylistic figures. There are two main kinds of
figures: (1) those of diction, which pertain to the location and
grouping of individual words, and (2) those of thought, the

forms in which types of expression are conveyed, such as questions, interjections, or oaths. In accounting for their function ancient rhetoricians often described them as "ornaments," a term distasteful particularly to moderns as being suggestive of frivolity or even deviousness. The Roman orator, Cicero, accepted the term "ornaments" to describe them, but he also employed a metaphor which lends a better notion of their importance. Cicero called figures the "lights" of speech. If we interpret him correctly, he meant that figures, like lights, have a tendency to call attention to themselves and consequently assist the immediate perception of the orator's remarks. Rhetoricians have cataloged over two hundred stylistic figures, many of which can be found in *On the Crown*. The present discussion, however, will confine itself to those figures which, either because of their prominence or uniqueness, contributed to the distinction of Demosthenes' style.

Of the diction figures in the oration the most important and typical of Demosthenes are figures of repetition. Synonymy, the prolonging of an ideal by repeating it in synonymous terms, is especially a trademark of the Demosthenic style. As many as four synonyms may be found in one passage, such as "spite, malice, abuse, dirt, and everything of that sort" (12), and "right or patriotic or just" (13). For the most part, the synonyms appear in doublets, "spite and envy" (13), "grave and severe" (14), "clearly and precisely" (40). The degree of synonymy varies from groups in which the words are closely alike in meaning, to groups where the correspondence is rather loose. The former type with such doublets as "assistants and accomplices" (61) or "her pride and her dignity" (63) seems to serve no other purpose than to prolong the thought for the sake of emphasis. The latter type, however, reveals an attempt to articulate or to refine an idea. One of the two synonyms may be more specific than the other, as is the case with "crimes and venalities" (20) where "venalities" indicates the nature of "crimes." In other instances the parallelisms of slightly synonymous words present facets of a single general idea, as "spite, malice, abuse, dirt, and everything of that sort" (12) or "a crop of traitors and hirelings and men hateful to the gods" (61). In the same category of amplification is the emphasizing of an idea by denying its opposite, "your associate, Aeschines, not mine" (21) or "not now in union with the rest of the ambassadors but singly, by himself" (33).

The single most famous figure in the oration is a *climax*, or ladder, in which the last word of the preceding phrase is repeated as the first word of the next phrase:

> I did not speak, but fail to propose measures; I did not propose measures, but fail to serve as ambassador; I did not serve as ambassador, but fail to persuade the Thebans; from beginning to end I persevered and faced, without reserve, the dangers threatening the city (179).

Climax is rarely found in Greek oratory. Its use required the utmost propriety to avoid seeming affectatious. In this passage it is highly effective in emphasizing Demosthenes' persevering zeal for his country. A similar figure employed for much the same purpose is also found:

> . . . I was persuaded . . . that, in proposing measures, no one would propose better measures than I, that in acting and in serving as an ambassador, no one could act or serve more zealously and more correctly than I (221).

This figure is called *conjugation* in which the same words are repeated but in changed forms. The example quoted above shows a change from participle to finite verb (i.e., proposing-propose, acting and serving-act or serve).

One type of repetition is so frequent in Demosthenes' prose that it is called the Demosthenic figure—*anadiplosis*, the repetition of a word or phrase with added vocal stress:

> But it cannot, it cannot be that you made a mistake, men of Athens (208).

Often, in order to heighten the effect, Demosthenes inserts a short, parenthetical phrase between the two groups: "I was persuaded—perhaps senselessly, but I was persuaded" (221). *Anadiplosis* is seldom found in Greek oratory prior to Demosthenes. As an indication of its emotional force, one may add that it is found regularly in Greek tragedy.

Another figure of repetition is the *anaphora* in which each of a succession of clauses begins with the same word. It rarely appears in the speeches of Lysias and Isocrates, but Demosthenes employs it with great frequency, for example:

> In the trials of impeachment, when you voted to acquit me and did not give the minimum vote to the prosecutors, you voted that I acted in the best way; in trials of illegality, I was proved to advise and propose only legal measures; in trials when you put an official seal on my accounts, you further acknowledged that everything I handled was handled fairly and without a suspicion of venality. What name was it proper or right for Ctesiphon to attach to results effected by me? Was it not the name which he saw the Athenian people attach, which he saw the sworn jurors attach, which he saw the truth establish to the world (250)?

This passage is an example of Demosthenes' effective exploitation of a stylistic figure. It is a dignified and fitting conclusion to the argument (beginning 227) concerning the orator's accountability to the state. The two triple *anaphoras* recapitulate the main points of the argument in an ascending order of importance (i.e., *auxesis*). Although Demosthenes usually limits the *anaphora* to three clauses (i.e., *tricolon*), he occasionally adds a fourth (*tetracolon*).

> Instead of the Thebans joining Philip in an invasion of our land, as all expected, my policy, which Aeschines attacks, caused the Thebans to line up with you to check Philip; instead of the war being fought in Attica, it was fought eighty miles from the city at the farther borders of Bœotia; instead of pirates from Eubœa plundering and pillaging, the side of Attica on the sea enjoyed peace throughout the war; instead of Philip seizing Byzantium and holding the Hellespont, the Byzantines fought with us against him. Do you think, Aeschines, that the examination of these results is like bookkeeping (229–231)?

Special piquancy is gained by *anaphora* in this quotation, since it is Demosthenes' rebuttal of Aeschines' accounting simile. The *anaphora* causes Demosthenes to appear as his own accountant calling out the credits and debits.

Demosthenes exploits the function of diction figures to the fullest. But the real impact of his oratory lies not so much in its well-turned phrases as in its ability to arouse a multitude of emotional responses. We learn from Aeschines that Demosthenes' presence on the podium was far from calm and that his gestures were often violent. His manner of delivery, which we cannot observe, was largely responsible for the excitement generated in his audience; but evidence of his emotional impact is transmitted in his writings through the thought figures. As a complement to the figure of diction, which adds nuance to the meaning, the thought figure provides emotional tone, such as doubt, indignation, pride, or hatred. Cicero said that almost no place in Demosthenes' oratory was without figures of thought. Certainly this is true of *On the Crown.*

Questions abound in the oration including almost every major type recognized by the rhetoricians. Broadly speaking, they fall into four main categories—*erotema, ætiologia, hypophora* and *aporia.* The first, *erotema,* or rhetorical question, occurs when the speaker poses a question not to obtain information but to place his opponent on the defensive, to express amazement, to arouse hatred or pity. Demosthenes regularly uses it in groups of three or more questions as a method of bombarding Aeschines with invectives:

> What do you and yours have to do with "Virtue," you scum? How can you distinguish the noble from the ignoble? Where did you get this knowledge? How can you claim it? What right have you to mention "Education" (128)?

To increase the effect, the orator combines his rhetorical question with *anaphora*:

> Why then, miserable man, do you make malicious accusations? Why do you fabricate arguments? Why don't you take hellebore to cure your madness (121)?

In *ætiologia* the speaker addresses the question to himself and then provides the answer:

> What was the duty of the patriotic citizen, what the duty of the man whose action for his country was based on forethought, zeal, and justice? Was it not to gain Eubœa for Attica as a shield against attack from the sea, to gain Bœotia against attack from the plains, to gain the states on your southwestern borders against attack from the places in the Peloponnese? Was it not to ensure that provisions of grain would be shipped along friendly coasts until they reached Peiraios? Was it not to secure some of

these areas, Prokonnesos, the Chersonese, Tenedos, by sending troops to help them and by advising and proposing such measures; to make other areas, Byzantium, Abydos, Eubœa, dependable friends and allies? Was it not to cut off the principal resources of the enemy and to supply resources which Athens lacked (301–302)?

Aetiologia exerts a strongly persuasive effect. Hermogenes, a rhetorician who greatly admired Demosthenes, observed that the figure wins the confidence of the audience, since the orator who asks himself must be certain of his case. On the other hand, *hypophora* is a figure whereby the orator asks his adversary what can be said in his favor and then counters with his own refutation:

> What purpose could you have had in sending ambassadors at that stage of the crisis? Peace? It was available to everybody. War? The topic of your own deliberations was peace (24).

Finally *aporia* is the figure by which the orator appears to be at a loss of what to say, or where to begin, or how to say it. Demosthenes employs it effectively in this example: "Then, you— what is the proper word to describe you?" (22)

A distinctive characteristic of *On the Crown* is the use of exclamations and formulaic oaths. Interjections like "Earth and the gods" (139), or "by Herakles and all the gods" (294), rare in the speeches of Demosthenes' predecessors and contemporaries, are regularly encountered in his political orations. They offer further proof of the orator's constant quest for the grand effect, particularly as Greek tragedy and epic were lavish in using them. *On the Crown* is unique, even in the collection of Demosthenes' speeches, for its religious fervor. It begins and ends with prayers, and it contains expressions strongly reminiscent of ritual, like this vow:

> I swear it by your ancestors in the front lines at Marathon, by those who stood at Plataia, by your naval men at Salamis and Artemisium and by many others who lie in public tombs, good men, all of them, whom the city buried because it thought them worthy of the same honor, not only those of them who were successful and victorious (208).

The oath, expanded by the formulaic *anaphora*, gains religious intensity from its enumeration of the martyrs to Athenian ideals. Demosthenes' audience, ever conscious of its glorious past, could not have remained unmoved by its recollection.

Other figures are important more for subtlety than for emotional intensity. We shall mention only three which are especially prominent in the oration—*paraleipsis, aposiopesis, epidiorthosis. Paraleipsis* is the expressed intention of the speaker not to discuss certain things which he, nevertheless, mentions in passing:

> I would not even provide evidence for my actions, whether ransoming some citizens from the enemy, whether assisting others with dowries for their daughters, nothing like this (268).

It has the advantage of impressing the audience with the abundance of testimony in the speaker's favor, while at the same time his reluctance to utter it ingratiates him. A related figure is *aposiopesis*, the sudden breaking off in a line of thought partly out of pathos, where anger or some other emotion is projected, partly out of modesty, where the speaker is reluctant to utter something offensive:

> . . . it is not the same thing for me to fail to achieve your good will and for him to fail in his prosecution, while for me—I don't wish to say anything offensive at the beginning of my speech, but he accuses me from a superior position (3).

Many other thought figures whose aim appears to be that of subtlety are employed. That Demosthenes has used them shows that he was at home with all of the devices of oratory necessary to his profession.

His selection of stylistic figures is characterized by a preference for emphasis and forcefulness. Figures of repetition, such as synonymy, *anaphora,* and *anadiplosis*, signalize a desire to prolong and to refine expression. Thought figures of emotional intensity are predominant. They range from the bitter invective of *erotema* to the religious fervor of oaths and formulaic vows recalling Greek tragedy.

From a discussion of the language, phrasing, and stylistic figures of *On the Crown* three major characteristics emerge. The first is range. In the use of language Demosthenes reveals greater freedom and facility than any of his predecessors or contemporaries. In phrasing he combines and adapts to his own style the Gorgian, Lysian, and Isocratean modes. His stylistic figures include not only the usual traditional devices but also forms of expression associated with poetry. The second characteristic is control. In spite of the oration's extensive range, everywhere the orator is the master. Through recurrent language each of the main characters mentioned in the speech is invested with consistent traits and associations. Control is also seen in the phrasing, where Demosthenes avoids the excesses of his predecessors while at the same time he adapts their best qualities for his own purposes. The third characteristic is one which epitomizes Demosthenic oratory—force. Through the selective and controlled use of language, phrasing, and stylistic figures, Demosthenes impresses a thought or arouses an emotion so that the reader perceives and feels with the orator. So great is the mesmeric effect of *On the Crown* that a special effort is required to resist its charm. Style is thus one of Demosthenes' main instruments of persuasion.

Selected Bibliography

BOOKS

Adams, C. D. *Demosthenes and His Influence*. New York: Longmans, Green, 1927.

Aeschines. *Discours [par] Eschines*, texte établi et traduit par Victor Martin et Guy de Budé. Paris: Les Belles lettres, 1962.

————. *The Speeches of Aeschines*, trans. by C. D. Adams. London: Heineman, 1919.

Blass, Friedrich. *Die attische Beredsamkeit*, 3 vols. Leipzig, 1874–93.

Brédif, Louis. *Political Eloquence in Greece: Demosthenes*, trans. by M. J. MacMahon. Chicago: S. C. Griggs, 1881.

Clemenceau, Georges. *Demosthenes*, trans. by Charles Miner Thompson. London: Hodder and Stoughton, 1924.

Cloché, Paul. *Démosthène et la fin de la democratie athénienne.* Paris: Payot, 1937.

Demosthenes. *The Oration of Demosthenes On the Crown*, trans. by F. P. Simpson, rhetorical commentary by F. P. Donnelly. New York: Fordham University Press, 1941.

Drerup, Engelbert. *Demosthenes im Urteile des Altertums*. Würzburg, 1923.

Fox, Wilhelm. *Die Kranzrede des Demosthenes*. Leipzig, 1880.

Goodwin, William W. *Demosthenes on the Crown*, with critical and explanatory notes. Cambridge, Eng.: Cambridge University Press, 1901.

Jaeger, W. *Demosthenes, the Origin and Growth of his Policy*. New York: Octagon Books, 1963.

Mathieu, Georges. *Démosthène: l'homme et l'œuvre*. Paris: Boivan, 1948.

Pickard-Cambridge, A. W. *Demosthenes and the Last Days of Greek Freedom*. New York: G. P. Putnam, 1914.

Schaefer, Arnold. *Demosthenes und seine Zeit*. Leipzig: Teubner, 1858.

Sinclair, T. A. *A History of Classical Greek Literature: From Homer to Aristotle*. New York: Collier Books, 1962.

Treves, Piero. *Demostene: L'Orazione per la corona*. Milan: Signorelli, 1938.

ARTICLES

Bonner, Robert J. "Wit and Humor in Athenian Courts," *Classical Philology*, XVII (1922), 97–103.

Cawkwell, G. L. "Demosthenes' Policy After the Peace of Philocrates," *Classical Quarterly*, XIII (1963), 120–138.

————. "Eubulus," *Journal of Hellenic Studies*, LXXXIII (1963), 47–67.

————. "Aeschines and the Ruin of Phocis," *Revue des études grecques*, LXXV (1962), 453–459.

————. "The Defense of Olynthus," *Classical Quarterly*, XII (1962), 122–140.

————. "Demosthenes and the Stratiotic Fund," *Mnemosyne*, XV (1962), 377–383.

————. "Notes on the Social War," *Classica et Mediævalia*, XXIII (1962), 34–39.

Cronin, James F. "The Athenian Juror and Emotional Pleas," *Classical Journal*, XXXIV (1939), 471–479.

De Sainte Croix, G. E. M. "The Alleged Secret Pact Between Athens and Philip II Concerning Amphipolis and Pydna," *Classical Quarterly*, XIII (1963), 110–119.

Dorjahn, Alfred P. "Extenuating Circumstances in Athenian Courts," *Classical Philology*, XXV (1930), 162–172.

————. "Extemporaneous Elements in Certain Orations and the Prooemia of Demosthenes," *American Journal of Philology*, LXXVIII (1957), 287–296.

Index

Index

Abstract terms, 190
Ad hominem attack, 162
Aeschines, vii, 3, 11, 13, 18, 21, 33, 44–46, 49–52, 60–67, 69, 70, 72–75, 78, 81–92, 95, 97–100, 102–106, 110, 112–120, 122, 129, 131–133, 141, 142, 147, 148, 150–155, 159–169, 171–173, 176–181, 184, 195
Aetiologia 196
Against Androtion, 34, 35, 38, 39
Against Aristocrates, 33, 34
Against Callicles, 31
Against Ctesiphon, 33, 47, 48, 53, 180
Against Leptines, 34, 35, 38, 39, 41
Against Midas, 33
Against Timarchus, 48
Against Timocrates, 34
Alcidamus, 5
Alexander, 7, 17, 19, 20, 23, 52, 56, 70, 113, 118, 123, 149–151, 156, 158, 168, 169

Amphictyonic Council, 50, 51, 88–91, 123, 141, 154
Amphissians, 89, 90, 141, 154
Amplitude, 191
Anadiplosis, 194, 198
Analysis, 133
Anaphora, 194–196, 198
Androtion, 36, 37, 39, 45
Antipater, 23–25, 27, 150–152
Antiphon, 12
Antithesis, 182, 183, 186, 192
    of Gorgias, 183–184
Aphobus, 29–31, 37
Apollodorus, 12, 32, 33
Aporia, 196, 197
Aposiopesis, 198
Appeal, 131, 132
Areopagus, 22
Argument from probability, 30, 31
Arguments, 129, 164–165
Aristophanes, 177–178
Aristophon, 33, 39, 92, 103
Aristotle, ix, 127, 130
Arrangement, 134, 165–167

Contributors

JAMES J. MURPHY, general editor, is Chairman of the Department of Rhetoric at the University of California at Davis.

GEORGE KENNEDY is Chairman of the Department of Classics at the University of North Carolina.

DONOVAN J. OCHS is a member of the Department of Rhetoric at the University of California at Davis.

JOHN J. KEANEY, translator of *On the Crown*, is a member of the Department of Classics at Princeton University.

JON M. ERICSON is Chairman of the Department of Speech at Central Washington State College at Ellensburg.

The late FRANCIS P. DONNELLY, S.J., was for many years a member of the faculty of Fordham University.

CHARLES RANN KENNEDY, a prominent nineteenth-century scholar, translated Demosthenes' speeches for the well-known Bohn Classical Library.

GALEN O. ROWE is a member of the Department of Classics at the State University of Iowa at Iowa City.